NEW BRUNSWICK

A COLOUR GUIDEBOOK

Edited by Marianne and H.A. Eiselt

FORMAC PUBLISHING COMPANY LIMITED
HALIFAX

CONTENTS

The development and pre-publication work on this project was funded in part by the Canada/Nova Scotia Cooperation Agreement on Cultural Development.
Formac Publishing acknowledges the support of the Nova Scotia Department of Education and Culture in the development of writing and publishing in Canada.

Canadian Cataloguing in Publication Data
Eiselt, Marianne.
New Brunswick
2nd ed.
(Colourguide Series)
Includes index.
ISBN 0-88780-344-X
1. New Brunswick — Guidebooks. I. Eiselt, Horst A., 1950- . II. Title III. Series
FC2457.E57 1996   917.15'1044   C96-950093-9   F1042.E57 1996

Formac Publishing Company Limited
5502 Atlantic Street
Halifax B3H 1G4
Printed in Canada

Distributed in the United States by:
Seven Hills Book Distributors
49 Central Avenue
Cinncinnati, Ohio   45202

Distributed in the United Kingdom by:
Springfield Books
Norman Road, Denby Dale
Huddersfield, W Yorkshire
England   HD8 8TH

CONTENTS

3

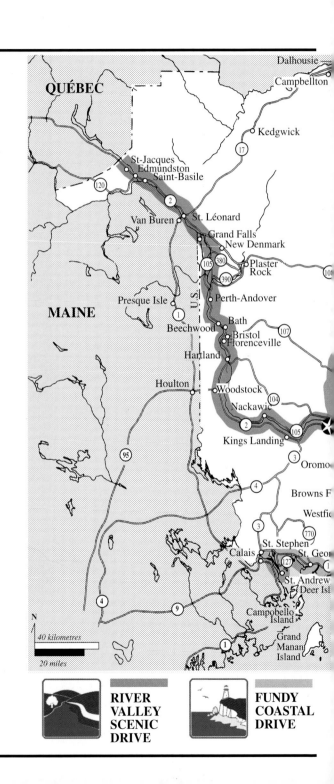

RIVER VALLEY SCENIC DRIVE

FUNDY COASTAL DRIVE

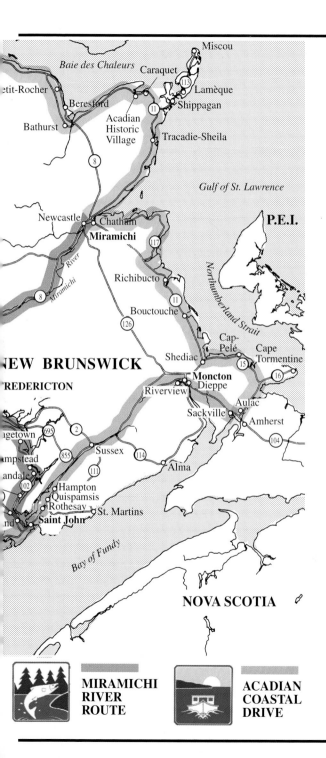

MIRAMICHI
RIVER
ROUTE

ACADIAN
COASTAL
DRIVE

INTRODUCING NEW BRUNSWICK

HOPEWELL ROCKS

New Brunswick is the gateway to the four Atlantic provinces — a 73,437 sq. km (28,354 sq. mi.) cornerstone linking Maine and New England to the south and Quebec and central Canada to the north. It is perhaps Canada's best-kept secret, the province many drive through, intent on other destinations.

Alas, the secret may already be out. More and more cruise ships are including Saint John and St. Andrews as ports of call. American yachtsmen have already discovered the St. John. Travellers with exercise in mind are hiking and biking New Brunswick's smaller roads and byways. Thousands throng to weekend rock concerts on the beaches near Shediac. A different group of music lovers is found in increasing numbers at the widely acclaimed baroque festival on the island of Lameque, in the northeasten corner of the province. For nearly a hundred years, sports fishing enthusiasts have been heading for the Miramichi and Restigouche rivers in hope of catching a mighty Atlantic salmon. Today, they must catch and release, in order to conserve these rivers' stock. Now, many people come to New Brunswick for an entirely different activity: whale watching, and for this the southwestern corner of the province is considered to be the best whale-watching vantage point along the entire Atlantic coast.

This guidebook was conceived by Marianne and H.A. Eiselt as an introduction to the natural wonders and cultural attractions of their home province.

Starting in 1992, they logged some 13,000 kilometres (8,000 miles), taking photographs and writing informal but informative descriptions of New Brunswick's rich heritage resources — pioneer villages, museums, lumber camps,

parks, tide vistas, and festivals (Scottish, Irish, Acadian, and others). They followed the travel routes that are featured in government travel literature, often detouring to find interesting places and sites.

Marianne and H.A. Eiselt live in Fredericton, New Brunswick's scenic capital, where they are both on the faculty of the University of New Brunswick. The Eiselts are passionate hikers and photographers, and their interest in guidebook writing came naturally out of their travels. This is their second; the first is *A Hiking Guide to New Brunswick* published by Goose Lane Editions.

This book begins with background articles that briefly recount the history of some of New Brunswick's major ethnic groups. In the feature section, you can read about some of the things that are of special interest to visitors–outdoor adventure opportunities, fine 19th-century church architecture, and the province's culinary traditions and specialties. The third main section of the book contains chapters describing the four major scenic routes of the province and the attractions along those routes which Marianne and H.A. Eiselt recommend to visitors. Each chapter begins with a map of the route, and the places identified on the map are described in the pages that follow it. For detailed information on each of the attractions including dates and hours of opening, turn to the listings section at the back of the book. The listings are presented in the same travel route sequence.

Every year the province of New Brunswick publishes free guides that provide basic up-to-date listings of accommodation, dining, and attractions. These are available free of charge by calling the province's toll-free travel information line at 1-800-561-0123. Or you can pick them up from the province's many information centres located at all major points of entry, and throughout the province as well.

A distinctive feature of this guidebook is the "background" chapters, which provide concise histories of New Brunswick's major ethnic groupings, its cities, and its regions. The contributors are all New Brunswickers and experts in their respective fields.

Richard Wilbur, the author of the introductions to each of the four scenic drives and the brief histories of his province's three major cities, traces his New Brunswick roots to the 18th century on both sides of his family. He is a freelance writer and historian who teaches part-time at the University of New Brunswick and lives in the town of St. Andrews.

ACADIAN FLAG

LEGISLATIVE ASSEMBLY, FREDERICTON

LOBSTER VESSELS

Patrick Polchies, who wrote about New Brunswick's Native Peoples, is a Maliseet Indian who has done extensive research and writing about New Brunswick's first peoples. He lives in Fredericton where he manages a graphic design firm.

The chapter on New Brunswick's Acadian population was contributed by **Jean-Roch Cyr**, a historian who graduated from the University of Moncton and received his PhD from the University of Montreal. He has recently contributed articles on Acadian history to *Acadiensis* and to a collection to be published by Carleton University Press. He works as a consultant in Fredericton.

Benoit Bérubé has written the chapter on the Republic of Madawaska and the Brayons. Bérubé is a graduate of history from the University of Moncton. A resident of Edmundston, he works as a labour-market analyst for the federal government.

Wallace Brown, author of the chapter on the Loyalists, teaches history at the University of New Brunswick in Fredericton. He is a leading authority on the Loyalists, about whom he has written numerous academic articles and books. He is also a travel writer, and his work has appeared in many publications including the *Globe and Mail*.

Harold Wright is the contributor of the chapter on the Irish in New Brunswick. A resident of Saint John, he has written several books on Partridge Island and Saint John as well as a guide to the Saint John Bay of Fundy region.

Along with companion volumes on Nova Scotia, Prince Edward Island and Manitoba, this book is one of a series of guidebooks published by Formac Publishing of Halifax.

Like the other books in this series, you can use this book with confidence in making your travel plans for New Brunswick. The entries were independently chosen by the authors — no payments or donations of any kind were solicited or accepted from anyone in connection with this book. We hope you'll be surprised by the wide range of fascinating possibilities in New Brunswick, and that you'll enjoy reading about and visiting the many attractions that Marianne and H.A. Eiselt found on their travels.

— The Publishers

PEOPLES

NATIVE PEOPLES

BY PATRICK POLCHIES

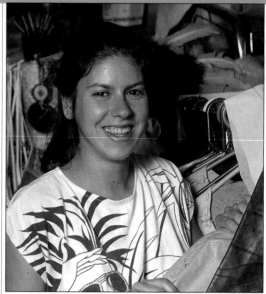

EARLY YEARS

Eleven thousand years ago the land sometimes called "The Picture Province" was very different from the forested valleys, rugged shorelines, and fertile fields that give New Brunswick its present nickname.

The geography and climate of the entire Maritime region was being affected by a northerly retreat of glacial ice which caused huge fluctuations in sea levels that continually changed the coastline. The land we know as New Brunswick was a sub-arctic marine environment dominated by mosses, lichens, and scattered clumps of very dense dwarf spruce trees — very similar to the northern tundra.

The first Native people to inhabit the region were the Paleo-Indians, a widespread culture that followed the withdrawing ice as it moved northward.

Between 4000 and 1000 B.C. the land slowly became more like the present landscape with a similar climate and familiar plants and animals. A number of different Native cultures began to settle New Brunswick. Early Native population movements, trade or exchange systems, technological preferences and widespread religious activities have been identified and sometimes explained by archaeology.

About 3000 B.C. a Native culture with ties to the East Central United States, began to travel and live along the western waterways of New Brunswick. The Laurentian People made tools from ground or polished stone, including heavy woodworking tools, distinctive crescent-shaped knives, and large, notched spear points. They were hunters of deer, moose, and smaller game, and fished the well stocked interior waterways for salmon and other species.

By 2000 B.C. a culture identified by archaeology as the Maritime Archaic People was frequenting the coastal regions of New Brunswick. This culture had technologies that included many stone and bone implements specific to fishing and hunting of sea mammals.

The Susquahanna People also arrived in the Bay of Fundy area from coastal New England around 2000 B.C. This culture manufactured Soapstone pots, chipped stone tools, drills and knives, and made greater use of interior resources such as deer and freshwater fishes.

The Meadowwood People from the Southern Great Lakes region appear to have made a limited migration to New Brunswick around 900 B.C. They are often credited with bringing the ceramic or fired clay industry to the area. Local cultures began to create ceramic pots for cooking and storage.

By 400 B.C. New Brunswick native cultures had thoroughly adapted to the various regions and resources of the area and were trading with other peoples as far west as the Central Ohio Valley and beyond.

The use of coastal resources, especially the collection of shellfish, formed the basis for the lifestyle of the Passamaquoddy People who occupied the southwestern part of New Brunswick along the Fundy Coast and the St. Croix River.

The Maliseet relied upon the interior resources of the Saint John (Wulastick) River Valley especially in good fishing areas around the mouth of the Tobique, Nashwaak, and other rivers that feed into the St. John. They also made their homes along the shores of Grand and Maquopit lakes.

Micmac people who lived in the Northeastern and Eastern regions had developed a specialized economy based on the resources of our coastal waters and the estuaries of world-famous rivers such as the Miramichi, Nipisiguit, and Restigouche. The Micmac culture also thrived in what is now Prince Edward Island and Nova Scotia.

CARVING BY
MICMAC ARTIST
RANDY SIMON

HISTORICAL PERIOD

First contacts with European cultures pre-date Columbus' voyage of 1492 by perhaps five hundred years. The Norse, from Northern Europe, appear to have visited the Atlantic region around 900 A.D., but seem to have had little if any impact on the Native cultures.

The abundant resources of the Gulf of St. Lawrence and the bays of New Brunswick were well known and already being exploited by European fishermen by the middle 1500s. Contact soon led to trade between Europeans and New Brunswick Native cultures.

Some items brought here by these fishermen were technologically advanced and attractive to New Brunswick Native peoples. Commodities such as copper kettles, iron knives, and firearms would have been especially appealing and were quickly adopted. The Europeans, in turn, were quick to adopt technologically superior Native tools such as the snowshoe, moccasin, light bark canoes, and the toboggan. The Micmac, Maliseet, and Passamoquoddy traded fish and the pelts of fur-bearing animals for European implements and soon depended on this arrangement.

The French were first to build permanent settlements in New Brunswick, a fact that did not appear to bother the indigenous peoples who — since they had no real understanding of the Europeans' concept of individual land ownership — likely thought that their purpose was to keep the trading routes to Europe open.

The next several hundred years brought rapid cultural change to the Micmac, Maliseet, and Passamoquoddy cultures through the advent of Christianity and an ever increasing flow of people from Europe.

Unfortunately, the Europeans, who brought the Natives a new religion, also introduced them to many new diseases against which they had developed little natural resistance; disease decimated the Native population. This may have been a factor in their conversion to Catholicism as their own medicines and techniques were ineffectual against such ailments.

New Brunswick's Native people enjoyed an amicable relationship with the French, who seemed for the most part to respect their autonomy. The two groups often intermarried and the first Métis (French-Indian) population was established.

After the Seven Years War ended in 1763 the British gained control of Nova Scotia, which, at the time, included New Brunswick. The natives were urged by the British to sign agreements in order to give a "legal" stamp to lands claimed by the Crown, and to alleviate the colonists' fears of attack by the Natives.

CARVING BY MICMAC ARTIST RANDY SIMON

These treaties generally guaranteed natives treatment equal to any of the King's loyal subjects so long as they lived in a peaceful manner. Large tracts of land were to be "held in trust" by the Crown for exclusive use by Natives. They were also guaranteed continued hunting and fishing rights, and access to trading houses where Natives could trade fur, fish, and game to their "best benefit."

Although the treaties seemed to acknowledge recognition of autonomous Maliseet, Micmac, and Passamoquoddy societies, they were quite ineffective in protecting Native rights. The colonial government was generally apathetic to Native concerns and did little to remove settlers who squatted on land set aside for the Natives.

Ironically many of the treaties drafted and signed during the early 1700s have become more significant in recent history, as they are often the basis of legal arguments used in New Brunswick courts to defend Native hunting and fishing practices, taxation claims, and land-claim issues.

By 1800 the fact that land had been licensed to or set aside for Native Peoples was of very little concern to most settlers, who did not understand the Native culture and

viewed their wandering lifestyle as vagrancy.

The increasing populations also depleted many of the natural resources that the Natives relied on to supplement trading. Micmac and Maliseet populations were soon virtually destitute and unable to continue their normal way of life without government aid.

Numerous relief plans were put forward by the government, most of them based on converting the Natives to farming by more or less confining them to particular pieces of Reserve lands. Funding for this plan, however, was to come from selling the best farmland on the Reserves, and leaving only the less fertile land to the Natives. Further, the squatters who were already living on these lands were unwilling to pay for what they already possessed.

Many Native leaders put forth petitions to stop such plans. Their efforts were, for the most part, ignored.

Shortly after Canadian Confederation in 1867 the Micmac and Maliseet came under new policies and conditions. The federal Indian Act was the basis for policy and control of all Canadian Natives over the next seventy years.

Maliseet and Micmac reserves in New Brunswick came under the control of Indian Agents who were appointed to administrate the various funds, lands, and resources of the Natives. Some of these men were genuinely concerned with well being of New Brunswick's Native Peoples, but others used their position to divert funds and resources allotted to the Natives into their own pockets.

The early 1900s brought small schools to some Reserves. They generally housed grades one to eight in a single room, and teachers often had fifty pupils at a time. Students rarely made it to high school due to inadequate elementary school education, policies of segregation at most provincial institutions, and economic factors. (Micmac and Maliseet children often had to go to work to increase the family income.)

The few who attended off-reserve secondary schools were sometimes forbidden to speak their own language, which was considered primitive. Racist attitudes alienated native students making it even harder for them to succeed.

During the World Wars many Micmac and Maliseet men served bravely in the armed forces. In the trenches and on the battlefields, they were equal to all, but when they came home, they were second-class citizens who were not eligible to vote in federal elections.

Until the late 1950s many Native communities in New Brunswick had no running water or electricity. Only in the early 1960s were Native People allowed to vote in federal elections and walk into New Brunswick's liquor stores.

KINGSCLEAR RESORT, KINGSCLEAR RESERVE NEAR FREDERICTON

13

1960 TO THE PRESENT

In the early 1960s, Micmac and Maliseet leaders began to make concerted efforts to address their people's problems. They used the media to create awareness of their situation and began to form organizations. Some met directly with members of the federal and provincial governments — one even managed to get an audience with the Queen. Such actions began to yield results.

The right to vote, and other legislative reforms, gave native communities more control of the funds allotted to them, thus encouraging autonomy and improved living conditions.

New Brunswick's 15 Indian Reserves, each with populations ranging from 300 to 2,000 people now have limited autonomy, although they still fall under the authority of the Department of Indian Affairs.

Most Micmac and Maliseet communities now have modern housing with running water and electricity, proper educational facilities and access to secondary and post-secondary education. Some of the more progressive New Brunswick native communities also have on-reserve medical clinics, recreational facilities, and even sewage treatment plants. Maliseet youth now attain higher education in New Brunswick and are increasingly represented in all professions, in business, and in the arts — where some have gained international reputations.

The recent acknowledgement of Native Peoples' mistreatment and the subsequent improvements in their lives have not, however, healed all the wounds of the past. Some of New Brunswick's native communities are still experiencing social problems such as alcohol and drug abuse. Many of these communities have developed healing programs that are delivered by Native social workers at on-reserve addiction recovery facilities.

ARTIST PATRICK POLCHIES

Such problems are often compounded by high unemployment rates, which many Native communities are combatting through economic development initiatives meant to create employment and more capital to maintain band services.

Recent political events have led to much discussion of the idea of "self-government" for Canada's indigenous peoples in the near future. New Brunswick's Native Peoples are combining the traditional values and cultural fortitude intrinsic to their cultures to overcome obstacles in an increasingly modernized world. Maliseet and Micmac children are taught to proudly retain their heritage and identity and to use these as strength for finding their place in society. The indigenous peoples thrived for thousands of years by constantly adjusting to the environment around them. This was their way before the coming of the Europeans and has been the key to their survival for the past five centuries.

THE ACADIANS OF NEW BRUNSWICK

BY JEAN-ROCH CYR

The Acadians are the descendants of the first European group to establish itself successfully in the present-day Maritime provinces. Today there are at least one million of them in various parts of North America, mostly settled in the Maritime provinces, Quebec, and Louisiana. In the Maritimes, especially in New Brunswick, they have largely succeeded in preserving their culture against strong assimilative pressures.

The French first used the name Acadie in the late 16th century to distinguish the maritime part of New France from the Valley of the St. Lawrence, which they called Canada. There was little contact between the two colonies; since France's economic interests lay largely in Canada, Acadia was neglected. The boundaries of Acadia were never clearly defined but included what are now the Maritime provinces

and parts of Maine and Quebec. They overlapped the territories claimed by England, and for that reason Acadia quickly became involved in the struggle between England and France for control of the continent.

Historically the Acadians can be traced to early settlements at St. Croix Island and Port Royal in 1604 and 1605; but their real ancestors are the 300 settlers brought from France to the region between 1632 and 1635. Generally, these early Acadians came from the west of France: Poitou, Berry, Saintonge, Anjou, Bretagne, and Normandie. The main settlements were made around Port Royal and the Minas Basin, but some settled at Canso and Cape Sable.

From the foundation of the colony until the British took over, the Acadians were victimized by external forces against which they had no effective defence. Raiders from the British colonies, a prolonged civil war between rival aspirants to local sovereignty, and the unending bitterness of Anglo-French relations harassed the colonists. But, as they persisted, their population increased, and although they were not as well served by priests and missionaries as

ACADIAN VILLAGE

their counterparts of the St. Lawrence valley, the rather loosely administered seigneurial system in Acadia did not impose heavy exactions on them. The Acadians gradually developed self-sufficient agricultural communities along the Bay of Fundy, where fertile marshes and high tides ensured healthy grain surpluses to trade for New England manufactures. They were peaceful by nature, maintained friendly relations with their Indian neighbours, and were deeply attached to their land. They tried to maintain a balance between the two competing powers by keeping a strict neutrality. Cultural differences emerged between the Acadians and the French Canadians despite their common French origins and their shared Roman Catholic faith. By the mid-18th century the Acadians had become a people distinct from both the French and the French Canadians.

In 1713, at the conclusion of one of the succession of wars between France and Britain, mainland Acadia passed permanently under British control. But the advent of British rule changed very little in the life of the Acadians. Their determination in refusing to take an oath of allegiance to the British crown perplexed their administrators but, as their peaceful intentions seemed obvious, they were allowed to carry on without disturbance. It was not until France began to make Louisbourg a North American stronghold and to strengthen other military posts in the area of present-day Sackville that the British began to take more interest in Nova Scotia. With the construction of Halifax and the founding of a British settlement there after 1749, the Acadians, who adhered to their traditional attitude of refusing the oath unless they were exempted from military service, began to be looked upon as a threat to British Nova Scotia.

In 1755, the British decided to drive the Acadians from their homes around the Bay of Fundy and scatter them on both sides of the Atlantic. There followed quickly the mass deportation of some fourteen thousand Acadians from their lands. It was carried out under incredible hardships; families were broken up and separated and no choice was given to the people as to their destination. Many of them escaped to the forests, only to be pursued relentlessly for years. Others found their way to France, Quebec, the Ohio Valley, Ile St. Jean (Prince Edward Island) and the Magdalen Islands, and, some time later, to Louisiana. But most of them were transported to New England and the southern colonies where, generally, they were unwanted and frequently were forced to move elsewhere.

With the deportation of the Acadians in 1755 and the capture of the French fortress of Louisbourg in 1758, Americans began moving north. The British authorities wanted to attract loyal Protestant settlers in order to prevent the return of the deported Acadians. In 1758, a proclamation issued throughout the British colonies invited settlers to claim the unoccupied Acadian farmlands. Many of these "planter" immigrants went to the Annapolis Valley in peninsular Nova Scotia, to lands cleared and dyked by the Acadians before their deportation. In 1764, the British government permitted the Acadian exiles to settle in Nova Scotia, providing they dispersed throughout the colony. Many returned, not to their farms, which were now occupied by New Englanders, but to the Bay of Chaleur, on the present-day border between Quebec and New Brunswick. The settlement of Caraquet became the focal point for the region. Other Acadians lived on farms along the lower Saint John River and in the southeastern part of present-day New Brunswick.

ACADIAN ARTISAN F. HACHÉ, TRACADIE

Following the American Revolution, thousands of Loyalists fleeing persecution in the Thirteen Colonies migrated to Nova Scotia and to other British colonies. They were instrumental in the partition of Nova Scotia and the creation of New Brunswick as a separate Loyalist province in 1784. Gradually, they built a new society in the St. John River Valley forcing many Acadian settlers to move further north to the Madawaska region and encroaching on vast portions of the Indians' hunting and fishing territories. Fredericton was created as the provincial capital and the town of Saint John became the major urban centre.

During the first half of the 19th century, New Brunswick had a significant Acadian minority, as did the other Maritime provinces. But the Acadians had remained outside the mainstream of the predominantly Protestant and British political and cultural life of the colony. An obvious social and religious division had appeared between northern and southern New Brunswick. Over 80 percent of the inhabitants of the southern part of the province were Protestants, imbued with British institutions and traditions, and in control of the economic and political life of the province. On the other hand, the majority of the population in the north were Francophone Acadians living in rural areas dominated by the Roman Catholic church. However, their economy, dominated by fishing, agriculture, and lumbering, was controlled by Anglophone businessmen.

In the mid-19th century, the Acadians began to feel a new pride in their past. Undoubtedly influenced by Henry Wadsworth Longfellow's romantic poem *Evangeline* (1847), many Acadians became increasingly convinced that they belonged to a distinct people. The Acadians clung tenaciously to the Roman Catholic church as the one institution that took an interest in their well-being. The church established elementary schools and, in 1864, the French-language Collège Saint-Joseph at Memramcook, New Brunswick. The college (which a century later became the nucleus of today's Université de Moncton) furnished the Acadian population with an educated professional elite from which the community drew many of its future political leaders and its sense of Acadian identity. Instrumental in this movement towards higher levels of education was the founding of a French-language newspaper, *Le Moniteur Acadien*, in 1867, which was followed by

TINTAMARRE, CARAQUET

others. This cultural awakening lead to a more active defence of Acadian political and social rights.

Around the turn of the century, the Acadians were one of the few ethnic groups in New Brunswick to be affected but not weakened by out-migration. Their reluctance to leave the Acadian enclaves of the region, the determination of Acadian priests to promote rural Acadian life, and natural increase were some factors in the rise of their percentage of the population between 1881 and 1911 from 17 to 28 percent.

Population expansion coincided with a resurgence of group consciousness, known as the Acadian Renaissance. By the 1880s, educated secular leaders, such as Pierre-Amand Landry and Pascal Poirier, were ready to define Acadian goals. To promote the Acadian identity, they held a series of national conventions, the first at Memramcook in 1881. During these meetings, the Acadians adopted identifying symbols to accentuate their distinctiveness. These included a flag — the French tricolour with a gold star added on the blue background — an anthem, and a national holiday — the Feast of the Assumption on 15 August.

But during the first half of the 20th century, many problems remained for the Acadian community. Issues included the poor quality of French-language instruction and the dangers of assimilation. Living mostly in the marginal areas of the region, Acadians were often poor, facing limited opportunities in farming, fishing, and lumbering.

During the 1960s, New Brunswick underwent rapid political, economic, and social changes after the election of the Acadian Liberal Party leader Louis Robichaud as premier of the province. His program of Equal Opportunities has benefited marginal areas of the province and the Acadian minority as well as all New Brunswickers. The Official Languages Act of 1969, which proclaimed the equality of English and French in the government, made New Brunswick the only officially bilingual province of Canada.

BAROQUE MUSIC FESTIVAL, LAMÈQUE

After many long and sometimes bitter struggles, the right to French public schools was recognized in the 1960s. Today, New Brunswick Francophones also have access to post-secondary education in their own language through a network of community colleges and the Université de Moncton, which has become a focus of Acadian culture. Acadians throughout the Maritimes also have access to French-language radio, television, and newspapers.

The Acadians benefited from a cultural as well as an economic reform. In 1974 the Conservative government of Richard Hatfield brought into force linguistic duality in the services of the Department of Education which, since 1964, has had two deputy ministers, one Anglophone and one Francophone. In 1981, the government of New Brunswick adopted an act recognizing the equality of New Brunswick's two linguistic communities (Bill 88). A year later, the equal status, rights, and privileges of both official languages in the legislature and government services in New Brunswick were added as an amendment to the Canadian Constitution. In 1993, Bill 88 was included in the Canadian Constitution through an agreement between New Brunswick and the federal government.

Today, the Acadians represent approximately thirty-five percent of the population of New Brunswick which totals around 724,000. Ironically, the largest Acadian community today is located in Moncton — a city named in honour of Robert Monckton, who became lieutenant-governor of Nova Scotia in 1755 and who was instrumental in deporting their ancestors. The rate of assimilation among the Franco-phones of New Brunswick (8.7%) is lower than in the Acadian communities of the other Maritime provinces. They have achieved more legal recognition of their rights than other Francophones outside Quebec, but these gains could be reversed if assimilation accelerates and their demographic strength diminishes. The real challenge for Acadians in the future will not only be to maintain their rights but to make more gains towards complete equality.

THE REPUBLIC OF MADAWASKA AND THE BRAYONS

BY BENOIT BÉRUBÉ

NEW BRUNSWICK BOTANICAL GARDEN, SAINT-JACQUES

Madawaska is a geographical region, a provincial county with a fascinating history, and a shadowy place of mythical reputation. Tucked into the northwest corner of New Brunswick, bordering the province of Quebec and the state of Maine, it is the gateway to the Maritimes — the entry point of vehicles travelling the Trans-Canada Highway.

Just over the border into New Brunswick is the village of Saint-Jacques, a must stop. In winter, Mont Farlagne makes this one of the largest ski resorts in the Maritimes; in summer, the New Brunswick Botanical Gardens greets all visitors like a giant garland of flowers — a fitting welcome from the unpredictable "Republic of Madawaska."

This symbolic status suggests the special nature of the place and the pride its fewer than forty thousand residents have in their home. The republic even has its own trappings: its coat of arms was designed in 1949 by Dr. P. C. Laporte and is registered in Ottawa; in 1955, the mayor of Edmundston, Harry E. Marmen, created the Order of the Republic and made the mayor its president; in 1965 Robert Pichette designed the republic's flag, drawing upon the region's past.

Madawaskans are sometimes collectively called Brayons, a name supposedly derived from the response of Madawaska girls of long ago to the overtures of voyageurs who were just passing through. Asked what they were doing, they'd say, "*Nous brayons le lin*" (we're thrashing the flax). This legend is the excuse for a bang-up party and

21

cultural event — *le Foire Brayonne* — that goes on for six days and nights every year, in Edmundston (July 28 to August 2). The people of the region make the most of their specialness — partly because it's good for business, but mostly because of Madawaska's history.

Madawaska, according to one account, became a disputed territory between Quebec and Fredericton shortly after the colony of New Brunswick was established in 1784. Thomas Carleton was the colony's first governor, and his brother, Guy Carleton, was Governor of Quebec at the same time. Guy Carleton was also known as Lord Dorchester.

FOIRE BRAYONNE, EDMUNSTON

The two brothers may well have asked themselves: "But where is Madawaska?" Even more than today, it seemed remote, hard to clearly define, yet strategically located. Its name comes from the area's original inhabitants, the Maliseets, whose term *madouieska* referred to the white porcupine, which modern Madawaskans have also taken as their region's emblem.

The official recognition of the United States by the Treaty of Paris in 1783 had left the international boundary with the American republic unclear. The location of the intercolonial boundary between Quebec and New Brunswick depended on a ruling about the boundary with the United States. Madawaska thus found itself part of Quebec, New Brunswick and the United States. While awaiting the boundary decision, the territory had to be administered, land parcelled out, the forests explored, and law and order established.

The boundaries were eventually agreed upon, and today Madawaska borders on Maine, about equidistant between Fredericton and Quebec. Its population is the most bilingual in Canada, and Madawaskans are more French than 20 percent of all the counties of Quebec.

THE HISTORY OF THE TRANS-CANADA ROUTE

Crossing Madawaska on the Trans-Canada Highway, today's visitor is retracing a very old route used by countless and celebrated travellers over the past several centuries. Before the Trans-Canada Highway, this was the intercolonial railway route. Even earlier — during the 17th, 18th, and 19th centuries — it was the canoe route used by voyageurs and Indians travelling from what we know today as the Bay of Fundy. They would ascend the St. John River, making a little portage

around Grand Falls; then follow the Madawaska River to Lake Témiscouta, make a big portage to the St. Lawrence River, and continue on to Quebec.

People from all walks of life relied on this communication link: missionaries like the Jesuit Bérnard (around 1611); Father Bernardin who became lost in the forest and died there about 1623, and Monsignor de Saint-Vallier, the second bishop of Quebec. The latter left an account of his voyage and it was he who named Grand Falls. You can find in this town at the southern edge of Madawaska a new monument commemorating this event.

MADAWASKA WEAVER, ST. LÉONARD

Until the great colonial war ended in 1763, military expeditions also used this route, including one Duvivier led into Acadia in 1744. In 1755, two French officers, de Marin and de Montesson, left Quebec with a detachment of soldiers and reached Beauséjour at what is now the border with Nova Scotia, making the 500-mile journey by way of Madawaska and the St. John River in less than thirty days!

Acadian refugees fleeing the Expulsion passed this way. In October 1759, about two hundred Acadians en route to Canada encamped at Saint-Basile, just south of Edmundston. (In 1785, this became the site of the first permanent settlement in the region.)

When the war ended, this became the couriers' route. They made the trip between Quebec and Halifax in 15 days — 40 miles a day — for a wage of $50. Some of these couriers were among the founders of Madawaska: Joseph Dufour, Louis Mercure, Michele Mercure, and Jean-Baptiste Martin.

Following the Trans-Canada Highway from Saint-Jacques, the visitor soon arrives at the city of Edmundston, the county seat for Madawaska. At first sight, it appears to be a big cluster enclosed in a valley. At city-centre, near the city hall, you can see where two rivers join, and watch the Madawaska tumble into the St. John.

If Edmundston seems big, it is because it includes Madawaska, its twin sister in the State of Maine on the other side of the St. John River. An international bridge has linked the two communities since 1920.

From 1820 to 1842, this area was at the centre of another conflict between the United States and the British

EDMUNDSTON

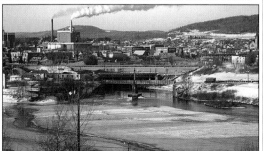

colonies. All of Madawaska, on both sides of the St. John River, was involved in a prolonged territorial squabble between the Americans and the British.

The thorny border question was finally settled in 1842 by a treaty signed in Washington by U.S. Secretary of State Daniel Webster and Lord Ashburton for Great Britain. Adopting the St. John River as the dividing line meant that parents and cousins, descendants of the same Acadian and Canadian stock found themselves separated by an international boundary. The Republic of Madawaska is really an international republic.

Edmundston developed rapidly after the arrival of the first railroad in 1878. Visitors will find it worthwhile to go along St. Sacrement Street and climb the hill connecting to Bellevue, which runs parallel to the main street but much higher up. This is a wonderful spot to view a good part of Edmundston as well as Madawaska, Maine and the international bridge.

If you continue the journey south from the centre of Edmundston rather than taking the Trans-Canada route, you will arrive at Saint-Basile. It is here and at Saint-David op on the American side of the river that the first permanent Madawaska settlement began in June 1785. The founders were a small group of Acadians and Canadians (today we call them Québécois), coming from Sainte-Anne (present-day Fredericton) in search of a refuge. The original family names included Ayotte, Cyr, Daigle, Dupéré, Fournier, Mercure, Potier, Sanfacon, and Thibodeau.

We suggest a stop at the Saint-Basile cemetery to view the gravestones of these original settlers. As well, visit an historic Acadian house and the chapel museum.

Continuing southward, visitors will pass by typical villages. Riviere-Verte and Saint-Anne (where an annual pilgrimage is held on July 26 to honour Jesus' grandmother). Immediately after this pious site, you can visit Saint-Léonard, the bootlegging capital during the Prohibition era of the Roaring Twenties.

In fact, all of Madawaska was the centre of major smuggling activities in this period. Legendary participants include Fred Levesque of whom it was said that he successfully smuggled alcohol across Edmundston's international bridge disguised as a papal delegate.

What does all this say about Madawaska? Is it a survival of Acadia? A corner of Quebec in New Brunswick? An annex of Maine in Canada? A clandestine republic? Here the myth is never far from history and history is hard to separate from myth. That's why the two should be mixed with a good dose of humour.

THE AMERICAN LOYALISTS IN NEW BRUNSWICK

BY WALLACE BROWN

LOYALIST DAYS,
SAINT JOHN

> Not drooping like poor fugitives they came
> In exodus to our Canadian wilds,
> But full of heart and hope, with heads erect
> And fearless eyes, victorious in defeat.
>
> —William Kirby

It is not generally realized that the War for American Independence (1775–1783) was a civil war. Many Americans fought for George III against George Washington. The perhaps one-fifth of the colonists who opposed the creation of the United States are known as Loyalists. Most of these "good Americans," as a British general called them, eventually made their peace, but at the end of the war a substantial minority, perhaps eighty thousand, went into exile. They were dispersed mainly to Britain, the Bahamas, the Caribbean, and above all British North America, which consisted of three colonies: the ancient (overwhelmingly French) province of Quebec; the small Ile Saint-Jean (later renamed Prince Edward Island); and the thinly populated (apart from the Halifax naval station) Nova Scotia. British North America was particularly attractive because it offered a nearby and familiar environment (at least for Northerners), retained the British political system (except for Quebec), and above all, contained vast areas of available land.

The Loyalists virtually founded English-speaking Canada, including the settlement of western Quebec, which as a result was split off as Upper Canada, the future Ontario, in 1791. However, the largest group — about thirty thousand — settled in the Maritimes, mainly Nova Scotia, which included the future New Brunswick. This hinterland wilderness contained only about three thousand pre-

Loyalists, largely Acadians and New Englanders, plus a small number of Micmac and Maliseet Indians. The concentrations of white settlement were at the mouth of the St. John River, upstream at Maugerville and along the bank opposite, and the Tantramar Marshes area around Sackville. Some fifteen thousand Loyalists, who arrived mainly from New York City in British evacuation fleets during the spring and fall of 1783, swamped the old

LOYALIST DAYS, SAINT JOHN

population, which led to the creation of the new colony in June 1784. The main Loyalist location in New Brunswick was the St. John River Valley and its watershed as far north as Woodstock, including the Kingston Peninsula and along the Nashwaak River. Both Saint John and Fredericton were founded in the process. As well, major Loyalist settlements dotted the Bay of Fundy from St. Stephen and St. Andrews to the Tantramar Marshes. A few Loyalists roamed as far afield as the Miramichi and Bay Chaleur.

Who were these Loyalists and why did they come to New Brunswick? Over the years, many New Brunswickers have cultivated the myth that the exiles were the cream of colonial society. In fact the vast majority were yeomen farmers, plus some artisans and tradesmen without special education — modest, ordinary folk well-suited to pioneering a new land.

KINGS LANDING

They represented a cross-section of colonial society ranging

KING'S SQUARE, SAINT JOHN

from the elite like Edward Winslow, a direct descendant of the Pilgrim Father of the same name, to former indentured servants and slaves. About half the New Brunswick Loyalists were former members of provincial regiments and their families: the New Jersey Volunteers, the Maryland Loyalists, the New York Volunteers, the King's American Dragoons, the Queen's Rangers, the Pennsylvania Loyalists, De Lancey's Regiment, to name the most prominent.

Another myth has it that all the Loyalists, nobly exiled themselves to what was immediately dubbed "Nova Scarcity," rather than submit to a republican regime. Although principle cannot be ignored, the truth is that many emigrés were simply scared to remain in a land where tarring and feathering Loyalists was a major spectator sport. Some were legally banned from returning to their homes; others saw opportunity outside the United States. All Loyalists were entitled to free land grants and government help in the form of food, seeds, tools, and other supplies during the first three years of colonization.

LEGISLATIVE ASSEMBLY, FREDERICTON

Some Loyalists' motives were frankly materialistic. For example, a group of traders at Penobscot, Maine, moved across the border to St. Andrews only when it became certain that the Navigation Acts, which monopolized trade within the British Empire, would apply against the United States. The lack of total dedication on the part of some Loyalists is illustrated by the fact that no less than six members of the first New Brunswick legislative assembly, which met in 1786, had returned to the United States before the session ended.

The Loyalists literally created New Brunswick, most fundamentally by performing the backbreaking task of clearing the trees, before settling the land. After the first winter of 1783–84, when many huddled in bough-covered tents or half-built log cabins and some froze to death on the Salamanca Flats at Fredericton, the majority soon achieved a moderate prosperity in farming, lumbering, and fishing.

The British government and the Loyalists set up the social and political structure of New Brunswick and most of the rest of English Canada. The aim was to avoid the "mistakes" that had caused revolution to the south. The elected lower houses (the assemblies) were believed to have become too powerful, so the powers of the appointed council (the upper house) and the governor were strengthened. The elite were entrenched through appointments to the council and government office and as justices of the peace in the counties. But the tone in New Brunswick was far from entirely conservative; the British never attempted to tax the remaining American colonies directly, and thus the essential early goal of the revolution was secured.

LOYALIST HOUSE, SAINT JOHN

The fact that the Loyalist rank and file would not meekly follow the lead of Governor Thomas Carleton and the elite was signalled by the first provincial election in November 1785, which resulted in riots between the two groups. In 1792 the elite lost its majority in the assembly.

Elitist hopes for an established Anglican church were also dashed. The rank and file were drawn to Yankee frontier revivalism — Methodism, Baptism, and other denominations.

The vision of the Loyalists as superior people has some truth. New Brunswick society was somewhat overloaded with what the 18th century called the "better sort," who contributed greatly to the new province. Christopher Sower from Pennsylvania founded the first newspaper; Gabriel G. Ludlow from New York was the first mayor of Saint John; Ward Chipman from Massachusetts was a distinguished lawyer — to name a few examples at random. And so even to succeeding generations: Peter Fisher, New Brunswick's first historian, arrived as a babe in arms; Sir Leonard Tilley, a father of Confederation was the grandson of Loyalist Samuel Tilley from New York; and the celebrated author Pierre Berton's Loyalist ancestors settled in New Brunswick.

The Loyalists — Americans with a difference — created a society in New Brunswick which, despite many similarities, is profoundly different from that of the United States. The obvious British influences are monarchy, law, and parliamentary government. From the start, the Loyalists offered a valid critique of revolutionary ideals and moral

absolutism. In 1771, watching the hysteria at the funeral of one of the victims of the so-called Boston "massacre" the Rev. Mather Byles (whose son of the same name later became vicar of Trinity Church in Saint John) opined: "They call me a brainless Tory; but tell me ... which is better, to be ruled by one tyrant [George III] three thousand miles away, or by three thousand tyrants one mile away."

New Brunswickers and most Canadians are much less suspicious than Americans of government. Unlike the rebels, the Loyalists positively embraced it. It had supported them during the war, transported them to new homes, provided land and supplies, given jobs and pensions to a few and half-pay to former army officers: all-in-all the benign promoter of colonization. Throughout Canadian history governments have intervened in people's lives more than in the United States. It is even argued that this partly explains why Canada has advanced public welfare schemes and a major public broadcasting system — the CBC.

The Loyalists began an abiding Canadian love-hate attitude towards the United States. The revolution had denied them their country, and now they shared the generally frustrated hope that New Brunswick would become "the envy of the American states." They took enormous pride in the accomplishments of their own modest province and the great British Empire. They cherished this connection as a shield against American imperialistic expansion. Fear of the United States has remained, and Unity of Empire has frequently been invoked in terms of Canadian nationalism — as in the 1880s, which witnessed one of several Loyalist revivals. Yet at the same time common origins have been habitually enlisted in favour of cooperation and friendship. As early as the conservative presidency of George Washington many New Brunswickers began to see their neighbours in a friendlier light. Many were happy to have their children educated at American institutions. There was bitter fighting in Upper

Canada during the War of 1812, but in New Brunswick it was business as usual. New England hated the war. On the St. Croix River border a committee of leading citizens from Calais and St. Stephen oversaw good relations, which continue to this day.

Although the Loyalists and their descendants retained political power in New Brunswick almost until Confederation, after the War of 1812 they were gradually engulfed by newcomers, particularly the Irish. But they had to great degree set the tone of the province.

Today New Brunswickers retain a generally sophisticated awareness of the Loyalists. Courses and research take place at the University of New Brunswick. The Fredericton campus houses a huge collection of Loyalist sources, as does the adjacent Provincial Archives, the haven for genealogists. Branches of the United Empire Loyalist Association (membership confined to Loyalists' descendants) flourish in Fredericton and Saint John. Each June in the port city Loyalist Days, with the meticulously recreated De Lancey's Regiment on hand, provide a varied celebration. As for museums the same city boasts the Loyalist House and the New Brunswick Museum with its fine collection of Loyalist artifacts. The wonderful Kings Landing Historical Settlement has several fully furnished and functional houses of the Loyalist period. Loyalist graveyards abound. Those in Saint John and Fredericton are special. Perhaps the most pleasant way to sample the Loyalist heritage is among the living. Visit the bucolic Loyalist Anglican Church at Kingston; in Fredericton stroll by the still inhabited houses of such Loyalists as John Saunders and Jonathan Odell; above all savour St. Andrews, which has the best collection of Loyalist buildings in the province. And, of course, question almost any of the locals to be regaled with stories of their Loyalist ancestors.

KINGS LANDING

THE IRISH IN NEW BRUNSWICK

BY HAROLD E. WRIGHT

While most New Brunswickers speak English or French as a first language, New Brunswickers are descended from dozens of ethnic backgrounds; the majority have Irish roots.

Even the name New Brunswick ignores the roots of this Irish province. The first governor was Thomas Carleton, a Protestant Irish. He recommended that the new colony be named New Ireland, but this was rejected in favour of the King's House of Brunswick.

The Irish in New Brunswick came with the Loyalists and continued arriving in the decades immediately following the Napoleonic War. It is the horrendous events of the famine years, 1845–47, that have blurred our focus of New Brunswick's Irish. Several historians, such as Professor Peter Toner of Saint John, have shown that most of the Irish arrived before the famine. Of the famine immigrants, most later migrated elsewhere; those who stayed usually had relatives here from the pre-famine period.

Several myths about the Irish immigrants have been exposed during the past decade. The image of the poor, drunken Catholic refugee from the famine is inaccurate. Professor Toner's extensive analysis of the 1851 and 1861 censuses shows that many pre-famine immigrants were Protestant Irish, who came voluntarily and were at least just above the level of poverty.

The first Dominion census of 1871 established that New Brunswick residents were 35 percent Irish by birth or origin, with its largest city, Saint John, being 60 percent Irish. It also revealed that most New Brunswick-born Protestant Irish adopted other cultural identities such as English or Scots.

The Protestant Irish allegiance to the Crown gave them common cause with the Loyalists. On the other hand, the Catholic Irish did not integrate so easily and sometimes became belligerent in their Irishness. Also, the decade after Confederation saw events that did not make the Irish popular. This gave many Protestant Irish political reasons to forget their origins.

Saint John is known as Canada's "Most Irish City," but it is only in recent years that this has become visible. Ten years ago the Saint John chapter of the Irish Canadian Cultural Association was formed. Since then Saint John has recovered a street named St. Patrick, studied the early Irish Catholic burials at St. Marys cemetery, reexamined the story of Partridge Island, and participated in the Belfast Children's Vacation. In March there is a week-long St. Patrick's Day celebration.

At the mouth of the harbour is Partridge Island, site of the quarantine station where all immigrants were held upon arrival. Nowhere else in New Brunswick so epitomizes the struggle, hope, successes, and frustration of Irish immigration. Because of its central role in the national story of Irish immigration, Partridge Island is known, with bittersweet irony, as "Canada's Emerald Isle."

Saint John's 1785 Royal Charter stated that a pest house was to be built on Partridge Island for those "obliged to perform quarantine." Immigration to New Brunswick grew rapidly after the end of the Napoleonic Wars in 1815. Professor Bill Spray estimates that between 1815 and 1865, at least 66 percent of immigrants were Irish. In the ten year period 1819–1829, the Partridge Island

PARTRIDGE ISLAND

visiting physician inspected 28,704 immigrants. We know that for the five years 1818–1819 and 1823–1825, over 17,700 immigrants, primarily Irish, landed at Saint John.

When smallpox arrived with Irish immigrants in 1830, Common Council reacted swiftly. In June the brigs *Leslie Gault* and *Feronia* docked — carrying typhus and smallpox. Immigrants from both vessels landed; their clothing and bedding were washed and the children were vaccinated. All slept in army tents until the pest house was completed. Council ordered that in future all immigrant ships would land their passengers so that they might be "completely cleaned and renovated." Constables were appointed to prevent the immigrants from escaping into the city. Vessels arriving at the quarantine station with disease aboard raised a yellow signal flag in the starboard main rigging. The ship was placed in quarantine for up to forty days to be fumigated and the sick cared for.

In June, William Marks and Agnes Murphy, Irish teenagers, died of smallpox. They are the first recorded immigrant deaths and burials on the island. When the station closed in 1942, six graveyards contained over two thousand bodies.

Throughout the 1830s, cholera, measles, smallpox, and typhus were treated at Partridge Island. In 1832 the lieutenant governor authorized the use of military force to enforce quarantine regulations. In 1834 Common Council prohibited all contact between residents of the city and those quarantined on the island.

Irish immigration peaked during the 1840s, and from 1845 to 1847 most immigrants arrived ill with typhus and smallpox. This massive influx of diseased immigrants created havoc in Saint John.

In May 1847, several vessels were placed in quarantine. By the end of May the hospitals were overcrowded, "the floors of every ward being completely covered to the very doors." More than twenty-four hundred immigrants lay sick, many on the open ground, some in tents supplied by the army. Over one hundred immigrants, and Captain Hall of the *Pallas*, died and were buried that month.

The famine year 1847 was the last period of quarantine anguish for the Irish. In 1854 there was a cholera outbreak amongst German immigrants, and smallpox ravaged the Russian immigrants in 1902. The island doctors remained busy. Dr. March reported that he inspected 74,906 immigrants and crew during the 1893–94 season. Most were Russian Jews.

In 1985 the Historic Sites & Monuments Board of Canada recommended that Partridge Island be developed to tell the story of 19th-century immigration to the Maritime provinces, highlighting the story of the Irish. In 1988 Partridge Island & Harbour Heritage Inc. opened an

TOP: CELTIC CROSS PARTRIDGE ISLAND

interpretive facility on the island. Tours are available, on a limited basis, during the summer months.

The Irish immigrants went to where there was a livelihood and in so doing have left their mark throughout New Brunswick. In the Miramichi region Irish lumbermen, labourers, and sailors played a major role in New Brunswick's lumbering industry. Irish priests served the Micmac, Acadian, English, Scottish, and Irish parishioners in the area. Generations of intermarriage have given the Miramichi region a rich mix of Irish, Native, Acadian, and Scottish blood.

In the early 1980s Farrell McCarthy of Chatham started the Irish Canadian Cultural Association of New Brunswick. Soon after began the Irish Festival on the Miramichi. In July the week-long event celebrates all that is Irish in New Brunswick.

Johnville, an Irish farming community five miles (8 km) northeast of Bathurst, was settled in 1861. Father Thomas Connolly purchased 10,000 acres (4,048 hectares) of land and named the settlement for Bishop John Sweeny. Little has changed in Johnville over the past century and a quarter. The charm of her people, and the lush rolling hills, remind visitors of the Irish countryside.

Scattered along the coast near Fundy National Park and Moncton are communities named Irish River, Irish Settlement, and Irishtown. Twelve miles (19 km) southeast of Sussex is Londonderry, settled about 1830. Petersville, north of Welsford and now part of the CFB Gagetown training area, is no more. It is now marked only by well maintained cemeteries of the early Irish immigrant residents. Many other Irish communities have disappeared, the only evidence of their existence being overgrown cemeteries.

Several communities throughout the province are named either for places in Ireland or after Irish immigrants. Some examples are Youghall, north of Bathurst (County Waterford); Walker Settlement, named after Samuel Walker, an Irish settler; Vinegar Hill, south of Sussex, for the scene of a battle near Wexford; Summer Hill (County Antrim); Shannon, named after John Shanahan, an 1829 settler; Shannonville, five miles (8 km) southwest of Dalhousie, settled in 1832; Newburg, six miles (9.7 km) northeast of Woodstock, established in 1820 by settlers from Derry; and Ennishone, four miles (6.4 km) northeast of Grand Falls, named for Inishowen, County Donegal.

Almost everywhere you go in New Brunswick you will discover small parts of Ireland, nurtured by Canadians who are proud of their Irish heritage.

FEATURES

New Brunswick Culinary Delicacies

Marg Routledge

Each New Brunswick season boasts culinary delights from the spring fiddlehead to winter harvested seafood. The province's varied climate and soil conditions, rugged coastline and high tides naturally provide her unique foods. Her innovative, resourceful people have turned them into delicacies.

BELOW: FIDDLEHEAD BOTTOM: MAPLE SUGAR TIME

Long before Samuel de Champlain suffered his first winter on an island in Passamaquoddy Bay, native peoples were enjoying the tiny fresh fronds of the ostrich fern. They are picked each spring after the freshet, just as soon as they poke their curly heads through the soil on the river banks. The early settlers called them fiddleheads because they resemble the scrolled head of a violin. This nutritious, natural gift is only harvested across Canada and the United States. They are also processed into top-quality frozen and marinated products available year-round. Boiled and served with a little butter and a dash of vinegar remains the favourite way to enjoy fiddleheads.

Rhubarb greets spring in tandem with the fiddlehead and stays on the market long enough to be combined with the first juicy, red strawberries in a pie, cobbler or crisp.

Many years ago, the native Micmac and Maliseets, in early spring, would draw off the natural sweet sap from the majestic Sugar Maple trees. The secret was shared with the white settlers and although it still takes up to 40 litres of sap to produce one litre of maple syrup, modern technology has improved the

evaporation process. Besides the top quality maple syrup, the industry produces a variety of gourmet maple treats such as maple butter, maple cream, maple taffy, maple sugar candies and granulated maple sugar.

The Natives also introduced the European settlers to fresh wild blueberries that grew naturally on the acidic soil of the province's barren fields. Although still natural, because the plants seed themselves, the crop is managed and harvested commercially, during late summer. Some of the annual wild blueberry crop is sold fresh, either at U-picks, farmers' or roadside markets or in supermarkets. Most of the fruit is processed (IQF, individually quick frozen) without added sugar or preservatives. For generations the wild blueberry has been cooked in pies, cobblers, pancakes, muffins, and jams. Today's wellness-conscious cooks also use wild blueberries in meat sauces, salads, light desserts and drinks.

The Spanish conquerors learned of the potato from the Incas, native to the Andes mountains of South America. Today, potatoes represent New Brunswick's largest horticultural crop and each summer, thanks to new varieties and new growing techniques, the first "new" potatoes are dug a couple of days earlier than the year before. The tubers which are harvested into late fall, are grown for tablestock, for seed (both domestic and export) but the greatest portion goes into processing. Baked, boiled, roasted, fried, barbecued, New Brunswick potato recipes provide dishes for every course, even a dessert candy.

The finfish and shellfish harvested year round from the bountiful Atlantic waters delight not only the palettes of New Brunswickers but of seafood lovers in over 50 countries. Although the traditional fishery has been decreasing, a growing aquaculture industry, has resulted in an overall growth in the fresh and processed (frozen, canned, salted, marinated and smoked) market. Lobster, crab and herring remain strong in the 'wild' sector

POTATO FIELD IN BLOOM

while the world-famous Atlantic salmon is the major player in fish 'farming'. Other aquaculture players currently include: oysters, mussels, arctic char, and speckled and rainbow trout. Looking ahead toward a diversified fishery, the aquaculture industry is doing research and development with quahogs, sea scallops, soft shelled clams, haddock, halibut, winter flounder, striped bass, eel and sea urchins. New Brunswick's original inhabitants, Loyalist and Acadian settlers all prepared seafood in the simplest ways, so as not to overwhelm its delicate flavour. These recipes for seafood chowder, freshly boiled lobster with drawn butter and salmon fishcakes are still prepared in the province's kitchens, but they share burner space with wonderfully innovative recipes created by modern Maritime chefs. Locally gown fresh herbs and vegetables, instead of higher calorie sauces and batters, now enhance the flavour of the seafood.

New Brunswick boasts the best dulse in the world. This dark, dried seaweed that grows on the ocean floor is harvested at low tide, and dried in the sun is part of what sets us apart and brings wandering New Brunswickers back each year to stock up on this nutritious snack.

New Brunswick's unique foods are a wonderful reflection of her rich resources and heritage. Served with a pinch of pride and a peck of hospitality they're as satisfying as they are delicious.

CHURCHES

GREGG FINLEY

CHURCH OF THE
ASCENSION,
NORTH HEAD,
GRAND MANAN

What follows is an excerpt from On Earth As It Is In
Heaven, *a book by cultural historian Gregg Finley and
beautifully illustrated with drawings and paintings by Lynn
Wigginton. The book is published by Goose Lane Editions,
Fredericton.*

This book explores the legacy of New Brunswick's
churches and traces the gradual shift in religious aesthetics
from the time of the Loyalists in the late eighteenth century
to that of the Victorians in the late nineteenth century. The
Loyalists worshipped in neoclassical churches of the
Georgian tradition. During the reign of
Queen Victoria, more and more people
began to attend Sunday services in
new Gothic Revival churches. By the
end of the century, all of the major
Christian denominations subscribed to
this architectural style.

SAINTS PETER AND
PAUL ROMAN
CATHOLIC CHURCH,
BARTIBOG

Of course, this architectural
transformation was not unique to New
Brunswick. However, the province
provides an early and, for the most part,
unchronicled chapter in the larger story

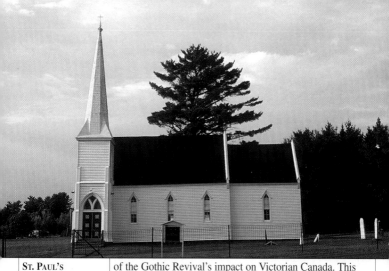

ST. PAUL'S
ANGLICAN CHURCH,
BROWNS YARD

BELOW: ST.-ANNE-
DE-KENT
BOTTOM: CHRIST
CHURCH, ST.
STEPHEN

of the Gothic Revival's impact on Victorian Canada. This Maritime colony was one of the first places in British North America to appropriate English neo-Gothic ideas about church design. New Brunswick's gradual acceptance of this system of Christian aesthetics involved many individuals and myriad influences from near and far, but the central character was Anglican Bishop John Medley. More than anyone else, Bishop Medley was responsible for introducing neo-Gothic church architecture to the people of New Brunswick. His Christ Church Cathedral (1845-1856) and St. Anne's Chapel of Ease (1846-1847), both in Fredericton, were the first churches in Canada to adhere to the exacting standards of the Early Victorian Gothic Revival.

Those who designed, constructed and worshipped in the Gothic churches of the twelfth, thirteenth and fourteenth centuries considered the buildings to be grand prayers in stone. People entered these Gothic edifices and, through a kind of collective meditation, they experienced the transcendent, a timeless phenomenon at the heart of Christian worship that unfolds across the centuries in the experience of those who desire God. It can be stimulated by the sight of evocative hues of blue, red, purple and green light streaming through stained glass; by the scent of incense burning and mingling with the fragrance of freshly cut flowers placed near the altar; by the sensation of textured oak or walnut along a window ledge and the hard, cold, stone floors where faithful knees bow in prayer; or by the sound of hymns echoing throughout the sacred space.

The relationship between earth and heaven is represented in the most characteristic Gothic motifs — the pointed arch. The arch points to heaven; it captures the aspirations of the pilgrim seeking to embrace the wonder of the divine mystery, to experience something of heaven on earth.

In 1850 most church buildings and worship services in New Brunswick were still inspired by the colonial American meetinghouse. In these simple wooden churches, worship was structured by a Georgian tradition brought to the province at the close of the American Revolution by thousands of United Empire Loyalists. A visitor who looked into the church through the square-paned, round-arched windows would glimpse an imposing three-decker pulpit dominating the interior.

The Georgian world view was anchored to a cluster of notions that stressed individual rationality, and self-sufficiency. These ideas were emphasized by the Enlightenment, nurtured in the colonial democracy of the young American republic, and transplanted across the border to New Brunswick. By the mid-19th century, the heritage of Loyalists and the American Episcopal Church of the previous century continued to be felt throughout the province, where modest white clapboard meetinghouse-style churches dotted the landscape. The neoclassical setting for worship was simple and dignified. For the majority of New Brunswickers, the

ST. ANNE'S, WESTCOCK

TRINITY CHURCH, SUSSEX

circumstances of worship were entirely Protestant, with value placed on the individual's capacity to encounter the Almighty through his or her own understanding of Biblical truth. The Bible was the ultimate reference for doctrine, piety, and order. Church life was locally based and often parochial, with much of the authority in the hands of the congregation. Religious truth was conveyed through the mind. The Gothic vision of society emphasized the heart. Realism and simple elegance were replaced by mystery, imagery, and artistic embellishment. Colonial American customs were superseded by British imperial influence; the classical myth was displaced by the medieval myth. Neo-Gothic architecture complemented a new emphasis on ritual and ceremony, in which Divine Mystery was sought through intuitive, emotional channels by means of music, colour, light, symbol, and sacrament. Beauty was treasured as an avenue to the Almighty. Both world views transcended denominational affiliation, and each was inspired by a particular conception of a glorified past.

BALTIMORE BAPTIST CHURCH

Five years before John Medley's arrival in Fredericton, Bishop Blomfield of London spoke of the need to extend

CENTENARY, SAINT JOHN
RIGHT: CHURCH OF THE ASCENSION, NORTH HEAD, GRAND MANAN

the Anglican episcopate throughout the empire. He pointed to the church's responsibility to provide for the spiritual life of British colonists and the need to convert native peoples. The Colonial Bishopric Fund was established shortly thereafter, and by mid-century ten new sees were created: three in Australia and one each in New Zealand, Antigua, British Guiana, Gibraltar, Ceylon, Cape Town and New Brunswick.

A remarkable collection of Medley churches has

ST. ANDREWS, NEWCASTLE

CENTENARY, HAMPSTEAD

survived in the cities, towns, and hamlets of the province, in centres such as Saint John and Fredericton and along rural byways in Browns Yard and New Denmark. Virtually every corner of New Brunswick has a Medley church: St. John the Baptist, Edmundston; St. Andrew's, Newcastle; St. Paul's, Sackville and the Church of the Ascension, North Head, Grand Manan. As well, the other major denominations were influenced by, borrowed, and adapted many of Medleys building principles. As a result, hundreds of Roman Catholic and Protestant Gothic churches were constructed, churches such as St. Michael's Basilica in Miramichi and Saint John's Cathedral of the Immaculate Conception; the United Baptist churches in St. Andrews and Central Hampstead; the present Wilmot United Church in Fredericton and Centenary-Queen Square United Church in Saint John. More than any other part of the architectural landscape, this collection of churches testifies to the Gothic Revival's dramatic impact on New Brunswick.

OUTDOOR ADVENTURE

BY LANE MACINTOSH

New Brunswick has always been a destination for people who want to get away from the rapid-fire pace of modern life by getting outdoors. Life seems a little more deliberate here. There is time to think about what you're doing, and time to do what you've been thinking about.

During the last few years, the province has blossomed as an outdoor adventure destination. But you don't have to be Indiana Jones to enjoy it. People from all walks of life who just want to get outside, take a deep breath and do something different will discover plenty of exhilarating adventures.

The province has developed a program called Day Adventures that provides many opportunities to enjoy the great outdoors in every corner of the province. The slogan is: "Adventures Left and Right, Morning, Noon and Night."

A cycling adventure in New Brunswick is like a journey through a James Herriot picture book. The narrow, rarely-travelled roads, and the excellent selection of country inns and B&Bs make it easy for you to create your own self-guided tours. Whirring down a quiet country lane, it doesn't take long for childhood memories to come floating back.

FISHING IN THE MIRAMICHI RIVER

BENNETT LAKE

DOBSON HIKING TRAIL

Maritime writer Kent Thompson describes many of the best cycling routs humorously in his classic book, *Biking to Blissville* (Goose Lane Editions). It's available in most Maritime bookstores.

Like any new experience, the first few seconds in a canoe or kayak are spent getting your balance — then, caught by the main current, you glide silently downriver through shadows of pine and spruce. Around every bend there is something new — a sound, a feeling, the sweet aroma of flowers and trees. Far above, like a dancer on a giant blue stage, an eagle gracefully rides the breeze.

Some of the more popular rivers are the St. John, the Southwest Miramichi, the Restigouche, the St. Croix, the Tobique, and the Nepisiguit. But there are plenty of others. Make sure there's room for your rod and reel too.

The most challenging time of year to canoe or kayak is in spring when rivers are at maximum flow. If you go in early spring, wet suits are recommended. In some rivers, low water during late July and August makes it slow going in places.

If you want to go sea kayaking, the northern and eastern shores have warm water, sandy beaches and, for your dining pleasure, tasty, just-out-of-the-ocean seafood.

Some of the most breathtaking natural wonders in the province, and in the country, are on Grand Manan Island in the Bay of Fundy. Resembling something left over from the lost continent of Atlantis, this mysterious island has become an international outdoor adventure destination. The Bay of Fundy's 40-foot tides are great for kayaking.

The late Melville Bell Grosvenor, former president of the National Geographic Society and editor of the *National Geographic* magazine, loved exploring the Fundy coast near St. Martins. Every summer, he spent a couple of weeks hiking and birdwatching in what he called, ". . . one of the most beautiful places on earth." High praise from a man who knew a lot about the great outdoors, and knew where to find it.

Many tours are available in the Fundy area. You can see whales — up close. And you can experience the thrill of hiking along rugged seaside trails watching birds ride the wind like valkyries.

Other excellent hiking and birdwatching regions include Bai des Chaleur, Northumberland Strait, St. John River Valley and Mount Carleton. The highest mountain in the Maritimes, Mount Carleton, has an excellent network of hiking trails.

MOUNT CARLETON

The most informative hiking guide about the province is the *Hiking Guide to New Brunswick* written by Marianne and H.A. Eiselt. The second edition includes the Fundy Trail, which is currently under construction, and the trails in Mount Carleton Provincial Park that connect with the Appalachian Trail. The Eiselts are passionate hikers and their book is a valuable asset to anyone lacing up a pair of hiking boots.

POINT ESCUMINAC

Every summer hundreds of North Atlantic right whales make their way to New Brunswick from the waters around Georgia. With only about 300 whales left on Earth, the right whale is considered an endangered species.

There are also whales in Baie des Chaleurs, which is often overshadowed by the Bay of Fundy as a whalewatching destination.

Humpbacks and blue whales visit the bay around the end of July when herring are plentiful. Tours are available.

Beachcombing is popular in New Brunswick. The beaches on Baie des Chaleurs and Northumberland Strait are warm. At Parlee Beach in Shediac (near Moncton), the summer water

MACTAQUAC

temperature averages between 19 and 22 degrees Celsius (that's about 66-72 degrees Fahrenheit). That's warmer than anywhere else north of the Carolinas.

To meet the demand of people interested in scuba diving, companies now offer diving lessons and rental gear. The northerneastern and southern coasts are prime diving areas, and each has its unique qualities. Inland diving excursions are also available.

A few days on a houseboat or sailboat is a surefire way to get away from it all. You can fish, swim, or just sit and look at the sunset. That's exciting too. Houseboat vacations are available in the lower St. John River system. Sailboat rentals and training courses are available throughout the province.

Fore! Some of the best golfing to be had anywhere can be found in New Brunswick. In Bathurst, you'll find a sprawling 18-hole course designed by renowned golf course architect Robbie Robinson. There are many fine courses all over the province. Some, like the course at Fundy National Park, even provide their own deer.

MACTAQUAC CAMPGROUND

Hiking... cycling... canoeing... whalewatching... the list of things to do is virtually limitless. It doesn't matter how young or how old you are . . . a new and exciting outdoor world awaits you in New Brunswick.

PLACES

RIVER VALLEY SCENIC DRIVE

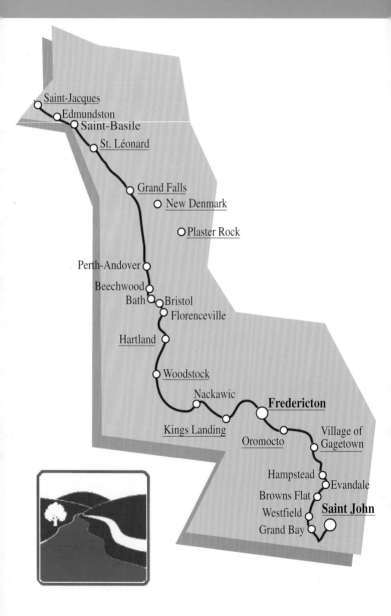

Saint-Jacques
Edmundston
Saint-Basile
St. Léonard

Grand Falls
New Denmark

Plaster Rock

Perth-Andover
Beechwood
Bath Bristol
Florenceville

Hartland

Woodstock

Nackawic **Fredericton**

Kings Landing
Oromocto Village of Gagetown

Hampstead
Browns Flat Evandale
Westfield **Saint John**
Grand Bay

INTRODUCTION

The happiness associated with the St. John... is a kind the world is losing everywhere. It proceeds from a life closely entwined with the river and with woods which are still wild and abundant with game: with family farms, small towns, neighbourly villages and plain people living with nature at their doors and not much troubled by ambition. Most of the intensely ambitious Maritimers emigrate; most of those who remain regard the living of a good life as more important than the using of a life for the sake of achievement. The St. John River country is old-fashioned; it makes you think of the growing years of eastern America before the pressures developed.

These impressions of the St. John River Valley, written nearly a quarter of a century ago by one of Canada's most distinguished novelists, Hugh MacLennan, might seem overly romantic — the nostalgic views of yet another Maritimer who went down the road seeking fame and fortune. MacLennan found both, but like so many who come back for brief visits years later, he wonders about the real costs of his departure.

Could he return again, MacLennan would undoubtedly comment on the changes wrought by the Mactaquac hydro facility 15 km (9.3 mi.) above Fredericton. Some of the rustic villages he admired now lie beneath the huge headpond that engulfed scores of farms and the winding river road that once was the main highway from Fredericton to Woodstock. A larger and more monotonous highway teems with all manner of motor vehicles, but the less-hurried visitors, intent on capturing the essential New Brunswick of today, can take other routes to discover much of the quality of life affectionately described a generation earlier. This 677-km (420-mi.) water "offers so much variety of scenery that a stranger ... encounters a surprise every twenty miles or so."

The first surprise comes upon entering New Brunswick via Quebec's Highway 185 (the Trans-Canada route), or

FREDERICTON

ST. JOHN RIVER

Highway 51 slightly farther west from Rivière Bleu. Both routes reveal how citizens of the Republic of Madawaska view the St. John River system. It is their summer playground.

The Trans-Canada follows the Madawaska River, a favourite locale for canoeing, boating, and fishing. It is the largest of many streams feeding into the upper St. John from both Quebec and Maine. Lake Baker, skirting the other entry route, has become the local cottage retreat. The tranquil world enviously viewed by Hugh MacLennan is alive and thriving in this distinctive corner of northwestern New Brunswick.

How distinctive? Enough to have its own flag and a special designation — brayonne — whose origin is rather hazy.

Madawaska's remote location, far from New Brunswick's other population centres, has also given the county its own momentum and outlook. And yet, Madawaskans share a common heritage with thousands of other New Brunswickers — the St. John River. No matter whether they live in the Madawaska high country (the flood plain that creates havoc to Perth-Andover each spring), the broader reaches around Fredericton, or the island-studded sections above the city of Saint John, their daily lives are shaped by the seasonal moods of "the river."

This applies most obviously to New Brunswick farmers, especially those close to the St. John River. From the high

rolling hill country above and around Grand Falls down to Hartland, potato farmers abound — and prosper. MacLennan would surely include them among his "surprises."

The upper valley, from Madawaska through Victoria County and on to Carleton, is the potato farmers' kingdom. Their neat, substantial houses line the main roads: in the yard, machinery designed for one thing only, the potato; close by the road and often built into a hill as added protection against winter's

POTATO FIELD ALONG ST. JOHN RIVER

blasts, at least one storage barn, more often several; and everywhere vast potato fields stretch over the treeless terrain, frequently reaching into the farmyard.

A massive factory complex near the riverbank above Grand Falls and a modern processing facility at Florenceville seem incongruous. The enterprising McCain family, not content with growing superior potatoes, anticipated changing lifestyles and eating habits and in three decades created a globe-girdling food conglomerate. McCain factories are on every continent, but their first plant and their head office remain in Florenceville, beside the St. John River.

GRAND FALLS

Visitors to Hartland — after stopping to admire its justly famous covered bridge — can take the "old" river road, rather than the Trans-Canada, and see some of the best and oldest working farms in New Brunswick, while getting a superb view of the St. John River. It is much wider today than in 1965 when the Mactaquac Dam's headpond was born. Some long-prosperous farmers were most unhappy at losing irreplaceable meadowland and river islands, for generations the summer pasture for their cattle. The majority acepted the inevitable and concentrated on specialties, including maple sugar products and apples.

MACTAQUAC DAM

Northampton, Southampton, Queensbury, Upper and Lower Hainesville, Brewers Mills, Upper Keswick, Temperance Vale; villages whose names evoke the "old country" — a term still used even though these yeomen farmers are seventh or eighth generation New Brunswickers. The heartland of both big C and small c conservatisms, they stick unswervingly to the politics of their grandparents as staunchly as they follow mostly Baptist or Methodist (i.e., United Church) versions of Protestantism. At the same time, they are quick to adapt to the latest farming methods and marketing demands. Every Saturday during the summer and fall months, their products are on sale at Fredericton's Boyce Market at booths staffed by family members.

Protests by farmers and other locals against the hydro projects failed to stop construction, but as a consolation, the government of the day helped Swedish interests to

SAWMILL, KINGS LANDING

build a pulp mill at what became the new town of Nackawic. Of lesser interest to locals — although it has become a major tourist attraction — an historic village, Kings Landing, was created from scores of houses and outbuildings that were moved shortly before the Mactaquac headpond covered acres of prime farmland as well as the old village of Jewett's Mills. The latter provided Kings Landing with one of the region's last workable water-driven sawmills. It was carefully dismantled and restored to become a prime exhibit at the new tourist development.

A short distance from Mactaquac is the charming provincial capital of Fredericton, with its legislative building and Beaverbrook Art Gallery — so close to the river that they were among many structures damaged by record floods in 1973. Well above the flood plain, "up the hill" as they say locally, is one of Canada's oldest educational institutions.

The University of New Brunswick began to take shape in 1785, just one year after the province itself was created. On February 12, 1800, it became the first college in British North America to receive its provincial charter, and in 1829 the Old Arts Building, still in use, was officially opened. The institution became the University of New Brunswick by a special act of the legislature passed on April 13, 1859.

Moving south out of Fredericton via the high-level Princess Margaret Bridge, car passengers (not drivers!) can feast their eyes on the mighty river as it sweeps majestically towards the Bay of Fundy. In winter you can witness Fredericton's "polar dip" action, where courageous individuals jump through a hole in the ice into the frigid

ANNUAL POLAR DIP, FREDERICTON

waters of the St. John River in order to raise funds for charity. And once past the roadside development so typical of most North American cities, travellers will soon come upon a less familiar scene — roadside vegetable stands displaying the products grown from soil enriched each year by the river's spring freshets. This natural phenomenon has a downside: most property owners have had to place their houses and barns on raised foundations to escape the floods;

most years it works. On the positive side, when the river levels recede in late spring, farmers move their cattle to summer islands, which provide safe and rich pastureland.

Time and technology have done their best to change the river, but one old New Brunswick institution remains intact: the free cable ferries. There's one just past McGowan's Corner, the Upper Gagetown ferry, which takes you to the west side and the old river road — a delightful and leisurely way to stay close to the river while viewing some of New Brunswick's original Loyalist settlements — Queenstown, Gagetown, Hampstead, and Evandale. When the paddle steamers plied the river (The last such service ended in 1947), passengers would often break their journey with a meal or perhaps a night at a local river inn.

The Long Point ferry takes you to the Kingston Peninsula, dotted with quiet picnic sites and excellent swimming locales. And once again, free cable ferries at Gondola Point and Westfield offer alternative entrances to Canada's oldest incorporated city, Saint John, where the river's downward current combines with Fundy's powerful tides to create the Reversing Falls — a sort of natural turnstile. When the river and bay are at the same level, boaters seize the opportunity to scurry up or down to their destinations. All too soon, the currents shift as the huge tides rise or fall, and navigation is closed for a few more hours — except for daring souls into white-water rafting!

FERRY TO KINGSTON PENINSULA

REVERSING FALLS, ST. JOHN RIVER

Novelist Hugh McLennan extolled the natural virtues of the St. John River a generation ago. Despite what human "progress" has done to it, it remains "intimate and very beautiful."

SAINT-JACQUES

If you believe that vehicles are just another tool to get you from point A to point B, better drive on. However, if you believe that a ride in a car can be something special, the Saint-Jacques' Antique Car Museum is for you. The museum features two floors of mint condition vehicles, dating back to the turn of the century. The collection includes a meticulous red 1906 Cadillac Roadster, and a less well known Russel, built in 1905 by the Russel Motor

SAINT-JACQUES AUTOMOBILE MUSEUM

Company, a subsidiary of the Canada Cycle and Motor Company. One of the most amazing exhibits is an 1899 Woods Electric Hanson cab. It looks like a horsedrawn wagon, has a top speed of 12 mph and cost $3,050 — a huge sum back then. Both the Hanson and a 1910 Detroit Electric ran on electricity; and a charge lasted for 40 miles. It seems that little progress has been made since then towards producing a viable electric-powered car.

Another car that was perhaps ahead of its time was built right here in New Brunswick. The "Bricklin" was a fascinating flop in the history of the automobile. It was a high technology vehicle made of acrylic and fiberglass, so it wouldn't rust. Other features included a steel-protected gasoline tank and gull-wing doors.

More than about technology or business, the story of the Bricklin is political. Malcolm Bricklin, a colourful Arizona entrepreneur, had tried to get the Quebec government to invest in his plan to build a car that he hoped would eventually replace the Corvette as the ultimate sportscar. Quebec declined the offer, so Bricklin turned to then Premier Hatfield of New Brunswick, who jumped at the suggestion. To him the Bricklin symbolized everything he wanted New Brunswick to be — modern and forward looking. He pledged support and even campaigned in the car. New Brunswick's Bricklin plant opened in 1975, but after 15 months and and an

THE MUSEUM'S ELECTRIC CAR EXHIBIT

$18 million loss by the government alone, the Bricklin project died.

You'll find many other intriguing vehicles in the museum, from New Brunswick governor L.J. Tweedie's sleigh to a Rolls Royce and the legendary Tin Lizzie.

An additional attraction is the New Brunswick Botanical Garden, across from the Antique Car Museum.

Designed by a team from the Montreal Botanical Gardens, the New Brunswick Botanical Garden is an artful center of natural beauty. Spread out over 7 hectares (18 acres), more than 50,000 plants are presented in several individual gardens. Small pathways lead you through the rose garden and the alpine garden, planted on the ledges of a small cascading waterfall. The shade garden is inviting for a rest during the summer's heat and the annuals, perennials, and rhododendrons are a delight to the senses.

In addition to the gardens, there are two arboreta featuring deciduous trees and coniferous shrubs. Stroll along a brook lined with flowers or take the short path through the region's natural habitat to the banks of the quiet river. The New Brunswick Botanical Garden is an oasis of color, perfumes, and music: Mozart among the roses, Handel in the rhododendrons...

The visitor center features seasonal exhibitions, a greenhouse, gift shop, and a snack bar that overlooks the gardens.

NEW BRUNSWICK BOTANICAL GARDEN, SAINT-JACQUES

ST. LÉONARD

In St. Léonard, the place to visit is the Madawaska Weavers. As you enter the building, you will immediately notice that this is no small-time outfit. Old-fashioned, yes, but not out of touch with business. The business was founded by Fernande and Rolande Gervais in 1939, after Fernande studied the art of weaving in Montreal. There was a big 50th anniversary celebration in 1989, and the weavers are still going strong with about a dozen looms in the shop and more people working at home.

Weaving on old-fashioned looms is still very much a cottage industry. Once a pattern has been chosen, each thread is led through a comb onto a warper, a big barrel-like contraption onto which the threads are rolled. From there, they are rerolled onto a smaller roll that is put on the loom. You can watch a weaver operate a loom with a so-called flying shuttle that weaves the weft (horizontal threads) between the warp (the lengthwise threads).

Upstairs, you get a glimpse of different steps in the manufacture of skirts, ties, and other products. Meticulous attention is paid to the smallest detail. Pieces of fabric are cut one at a time rather than in stacks, and each piece is fitted individually. A necktie, for instance, consists of twelve individual parts, sewn together with care.

GRAND FALLS

If you step out behind the Malabeam Visitor Centre onto a wooden platform, you will get a fine view of the dam, the huge waterfall, and the rocky gorge below. Here, the water drops some 23 m (76 ft) to the bottom of the deep gorge. The visitor centre provides background information about the geological and human history of the falls.

During the last glacial period (the Wisconsin Glaciation, 250,000 to 11,000 years ago), great ice sheets up to 2 km (1.2 mi.) thick, covered the land. In the process of their advance and retreat, hilltops were smoothed and the St. John River deepened.

Today, during the spring freshet, six million litres (1.3 million gallons) of water plunge down the falls every second! That is 90 percent of the volume of Niagara Falls.

Equipped with a small map of the area, available at the visitor centre, cross the Turcotte Bridge; turn right just beyond the bridge and then left onto Lover's Lane. This short walk towards the dam passes by the site of Sir John Caldwell's (1775–1842) sawmill. The iron ring just left of the trail is a reminder of a daredevil (an American named Evangeliste van Morrel), who, in 1904, walked across these falls on an iron cable. He even stopped in the middle and did a headstand before balancing to the other side! Continue your walk underneath the bridge to the La Rochelle building. Here, you can descend the wooden stairway beyond the store to the "Wells in Rocks" — large, circular depressions in the rocks, created by the erosive action of swirling water. From a parking lot in front of La Rochelle, you can walk along the gorge to its end at a picnic site from where you can see "Camel's Rock," a large rock that vaguely resembles a camel.

WELLS AT GRAND FALLS

The story behind Malabeam is an old Indian legend. A Maliseet maiden, named Malabeam, is said to have saved her people some five hundred years ago. The Mohawks had killed her father and taken her prisoner. They told her that she would be spared if she showed them to her

GRAND FALLS MUSEUM

peoples' town. Pretending to guide them, she told the Mohawks to keep their canoes together, and then led them over the falls to their deaths, thus preventing a massacre. A poem of the legend, by James Hannay concludes: "With a shout of triumph she went over the Falls bringing all 300 Mohawks into the dark abyss to death 80 feet below." They are said to have found the Mohawks' bodies, but not Malabeam's.

Visitors to the falls should not miss this interesting little museum. Its exhibits include historical photographs of Grand Falls' Broadway, around 1900 when it was known as the muddiest street in Canada, and pictures of the daredevil van Morrel. You may be surprised to see a gold pan, but some gold was discovered in the area, although it never amounted to much. An intriguing artifact is the rifle with a banana-shaped barrel. As the story goes, the owner of the gun used it as a walking stick! A plug of mud formed in the barrel, and when the man fired a shot, the barrel blew up. Fortunately, he wasn't hurt. Don't miss the collection of old cameras, some dating back to the turn of the century.

NEW DENMARK

FLOAT, FOUNDERS'
DAY PARADE

As you drive along the winding country road towards New Denmark, you will notice a subtle change. Names on mailboxes are no longer McKinley, Kennedy, and Duguay, but frequently Hansen, Pedersen, Jensen, and Christensen. Also, you'll begin to see red and white flags waving in the gentle breeze, but rather than the familiar maple leaf, their symbol is a white cross on a red ground. You know that you have entered "Danish territory" where Danish traditions are very much alive — especially in the village of New Denmark.

On Founders' Day (June 19), children perform traditional dances on a stage near a replica of the original Immigrant House. The painting on the back wall of the stage depicts the original Immigrant House and the newly cleared land with just the tree stumps protruding from the ground. It provides a vivid picture of how this place looked in 1872. Children in red, white, and black garb dancing the Shoemaker's Dance and King Gusta Skol evoke the rich culture the Danes brought with them, which helped sustain them through the hardships they endured when they arrived.

The first settlers came in 1872, lured by the government's promise of 100 acres (40.5 hectares) of good farm land for every male over 18 years of age. It is thought that the government hoped the Danes, by forming a buffer between the English and the French would serve to help reduce tension. Twenty-nine people, including 10 children, embarked

upon a steamer in Copenhagen on May 31. When they arrived in Halifax, the Danes boarded a smaller boat and continued their journey to Saint John. Here, they boarded yet another vessel, which took them up the St. John River to Fredericton, where they transferred to a small paddle wheeler for a journey up the river to the mouth of the Salmon River at Whitehead Flats. The final leg of the trip was a steep, rocky climb up a two-mile (3.2-kilometre) trail,

now called Lucy Gulch. A Loyalist settler provided them with a team of horses. On June 19, 1872, they finally reached the spot on which the government-built Immigrant House stood. This is where they were to live until they could build their own homes. They were each provided with 100 acres of their own land, but farmland it was not! Dense forests covered the area and clearing the land was the first priority. Their feelings are recorded in a publication of the Womens' Institute: "They had come from a country that resembled a gigantic garden ... they were like children abandoned in the merciless woods."

Unfortunately, the original Immigrant House burned down. Only a smaller replica remains as a reminder of the rough early days. It is part of the New Denmark Museum which is well worth a visit. Many historical photographs record the results of their hard work. Most Danes farmed near Klokkedahl Hill. If you continue past the museum and turn right onto the steep Lucy Gulch, you will arrive at the settlers' landing site on the Salmon River, now a small picnic spot.

PLASTER ROCK

Lumbering has a long and colourful history in New Brunswick. Much has changed over the last hundred years, from lumberjacks with crosscut saws to skidders and harvesters and other modern equipment. Processing the harvested wood has also become high technology. A good place to see it being done is the Fraser Inc. lumber mill in Plaster Rock, a so-called random mill, where different lengths and sizes of wood products are made. This is in contrast to stud mills which, as the name implies, produce only studs (posts of a specific size). This mill processes almost exclusively fir and spruce, and once in a while some pine.

Your tour starts at a "slashing system" where timber is unloaded from trucks. Here, the operator in a split second

must separate quality logs from waste — such as butts and tree tops. The waste ends up in a big drum debarker with knives on its walls, where it is reduced to wood chips and biomass products. The quality logs then pass through hot ponds, debarkers, double cut, and finally, edgers. (You can ask, during your visit, to have these mysterious terms explained to you.) In the production process lumber pieces are trimmed, graded, and finally piled manually. The last step is a planer, where lumber is planed and wrapped. Each of these processing stages can be viewed up close from the many iron walkways in the factory.

The kiln, in which the lumber is dried, is a separate building that feels like a sauna because the temperature is kept at about 40° C (100–110° F). The length of the drying process depends on the wood, but it takes an average of 21 days during which the water content of the wood is reduced from 80 percent (or even more in colder winters) to about 19 percent. Most of the time, the large dry kiln is stacked to the ceiling with lumber.

Another interesting feature of the mill is the filing room, where the sawblades are sharpened and new tips are welded onto saws. The shop is constantly busy as the saws require resharpening about every five hours!

The original mill was built in 1906 at the Tobique River; the present mill opened in the summer of 1974. Today, it employs 185 people, not counting the wood operations. The timber is cut on the company's own land as well as on crown land. Each day, approximately twelve thousand logs are used in the process. Recently, the usual practice of clearcutting has been partly replaced by environmentally friendly selective cutting. Today, all parts of the trees are used: the main trunk is processed into boards; the shavings and chips become biomass, (e.g. for animal bedding), and the sawdust is used as fuel to operate turbines. Wood chips are sent to Edmundston (Fraser Co.) for pulp and paper.

WOODSTOCK

Woodstock is a treasure of fine 19th-century architecture, well worth a walking tour.

Start your tour at the L.P. Fisher Library at 679 Main Street with its very beautiful woodwork inside. From the library, turn right onto Connell Street. At 128 Connell is the Charles Connell House, a large Classic Revival mansion built in 1839. The honourable Charles Connell was a successful politician and postmaster until he took the incredible step of issuing an official five-cent stamp in his own image! The misguided "ego trip" caused such a commotion that he was forced to resign from public office. Today, the Carleton County Historical Society owns the property, and the building hosts various displays at different times.

UPPER WOODSTOCK

Turn right onto Green Street where, at the junction with Chapel Street, opposite St. James United Church, stands a lovely white and green building in Gothic Revival style. This is the Judge Jones House at 119 Chapel. The pointed Gothic windows over the entrance create a distinctive character.

Continue on Green Street, with perhaps a side step into Maple Street, to see the exterior of the Woodstock prison, an imposing brick building that is still in use. Continue along Green Street to Elm; turn right on Elm and walk to its end, then turn left and walk up Grover. The large grey house on the corner of St. John Street is the Baird-Mair House (100 St. John Street). It was built by a Boston architect and features a variety of architectural styles. Continue on to a large white and green house on the corner of St. James and Grover. This is the Dunbar House, built in 1874 in Victorian Gothic Revival style. Its many nooks and crannies give it a spooky look, the stuff of mysteries (and horror movies!). A wolf-like gargoyle over the central dormer smiles grotesquely down on all who pass below.

Return to the corner of Elm and Main and continue the walk down Main Street. The Wesleyan Church on the right was built in 1883 and has windows with a notable cartwheel design. Its original spire was damaged by lightning and was removed in 1970. A bit further along is

CARLETON COUNTY
COURTHOUSE

the courthouse, built in two stages, in 1884 and 1909. It is
an example of Romanesque Revival architecture. Continue
on Main Street back to the Fisher Library, which concludes
your short walking tour through town. For a good
background on historic Woodstock homes refer to Allison
Connell's book *A View of Woodstock: Historic Homes of
the Nineteenth Century*.

As you approach the Old Carleton County Courthouse
in Upper Woodstock, you see a majestic white building
with elegant columns of Classic Revival style. What you
don't see is that this was a home for horses, cows, hens,
and pigs for no less than 50 years. The Old County
Courthouse was built in 1833, then extended in 1836. In
1909, the neighbouring town of Woodstock was growing
faster and insisted upon having its own courthouse. So, in
1911, the Old County Courthouse was sold for about eight
hundred dollars. From that time on, the former seat of
justice was used as a livestock barn, until 1960 when the
local historical society acquired the building. After great
effort, it was restored to its original elegance. Inside,
photographs depict the sorry state of the courthouse during
the first half of this century. H.R.H. Princess Anne
officially opened the restored building in 1986. Today,
visitors can sit in her chair and sign a souvenir document
— trying their skills with quill and ink.

The large courtroom was reconstructed from the
memories of those who saw it in its original state. It features
a judges' bench (the court system with a single judge is
fairly new), a prisoner's dock, chairs for the jury, and seats
for the public. As was customary then, the beams and pillars
look strikingly like wood but are not — the woodgrain is
painted on. The wallpaper is new, but has the colour and
design of the original. Behind the judges' bench is the
judges' room, with a horsehair sofa and a Franklin stove —
the most comfortable room in the house.

In the jury's room is a display depicting the work of
Tappan Adney. Born in 1868, he was an artist, naturalist,
author, authority on American Indians, and heraldist.

CARLETON COUNTY COURTHOUSE

Academics at Harvard often sought his advice on Indian folklore and languages.

Climbing up a large staircase with the original wood railing to the second floor, you reach the public balcony, from where you look down on oil-lamp chandeliers and the courtroom. The unusual looking black pipes near the ceiling are part of the heating system, which was reproduced from the original plans. The door to the prisoners' cell is now open. Here, accused and convicted murderers and robbers were temporarily confined. The last trial was held in this building in 1907.

HARTLAND

The town of Hartland, nestled along the St. John River, can boast at least two superlatives: with less than a thousand inhabitants, it is the smallest incorporated village in Canada; it is also the home of the longest covered bridge in the world, a National Historic Site since 1980.

The Hartland Covered Bridge is 391 m (1282 ft.) long. It was originally built without a roof by a private company, and it was opened on July 4, 1901. Being a private venture, there was a toll: each pedestrian was charged 3 cents, a wagon with a single horse cost 6 cents, and a double team was charged 12 cents. In 1906, the government bought the bridge, removed the tolls, and let the taxpayers bear the burden. By 1913, the wooden structure had deteriorated so badly that major repair work was needed. The bridge remained uncovered until 1920, when ice floes caused severe damage, requiring major repairs. A roof was added at the same time in order to preserve the wood as much as possible.

The Hartland bridge carries the sign, "No faster than a walk." This tradition dates back to the days when horses were the usual means of transportation. It was thought that the vibrations caused by cantering horses might make a bridge collapse.

Legend has it that every young man in the horse-and-buggy-days felt it his right to let his horse rest under a covered bridge while he stole a kiss from the girl beside him. To this day covered bridges are also called "kissing bridges." At last count there were still about seventy covered bridges in New Brunswick, but every year more fall victim to decay, accident, and vandalism. The magnificent Hartland Bridge remains as the finest example of a gradually disappearing tradition.

HARTLAND COVERED BRIDGE

KINGS LANDING

Kings Landing is one of New Brunswick's finest attractions, a place where people of all ages can gain a sense of the daily life of 19th-century New Brunswickers. As soon as you pass through the door to the historic settlement of Kings Landing, only tourists like yourself remind you that this is not really a 19th-century village.

When nearby Mactaquac Dam was constructed in 1963, a number of houses that would otherwise have been submerged in the headpond were transported to this site. All this was made possible by the combined efforts of many interested individuals, as well as N.B. Power, and the

governments of New Brunswick and Canada. Now, about 50 buildings form a living museum on a 121 hectare (300 acre) site on the banks of the St. John River.

Starting on your historic walk, you first pass a field of buckwheat and the 1860 Joslin House. You pass the 1870 Hagerman House, then the carpenter shop, where wagon wheels are made and repaired for use at the landing. From here, the road swings to the right and dips down to Corser's Cove. From the bridge across the cove, you get a beautiful view of the sawmill. This operational mill offers a look at 1830s technology. Its saw cuts a foot a minute, so it would take about three quarters of an hour to saw a full-sized tree. The boards produced here are all used within the village. At the nearby grist mill buckwheat is ground into bran and flour. The road ascends and soon reaches the King's Head Inn, a pub and a restaurant, where costumed waitresses serve plowman's lunch, catch of the day, and chicken. Once in

GRIST MILL, KINGS LANDING

TOP: LOYALIST KITCHEN

KING'S THEATRE TROUPE

a while, a few musicians gather out front for a number of traditional tunes.

A few steps further on, two horses walk on a treadmill which, in turn, operates an 1890 dragsaw. A short distance ahead, you usually hear the "clunk, clunk" of the blacksmith's hammer. He is frequently busy making small implements, which he gives away as souvenirs. Sometimes he sets down his hammer and takes up a guitar.

Past St. Mark's Chapel is the 1867 Perley House. Mr. Perley was both a farmer and in the lumbering business — a man of some means. His home's interior shows such Victorian influences as flowers, wallpaper, and a birdcage.

66

In those days, people customarily caught wild birds, kept them for a few days and then released them and replaced them with others.

Continue to the well-stocked store and turn left. At the end of the lane is the Ingraham House. The house was built in 1830, but its main attraction is the fantastic garden, where some flowers are always in bloom. Daniel Morehouse, who built this house, was quite a colourful man. A militia captain who knew how to enjoy life, he had enlisted men carry his bed and chest for him so that he would be comfortable in the field! He later became a justice of the peace.

GARDEN OF INGRAHAM HOUSE, KINGS LANDING

PRINTER'S APPRENTICE, KINGS LANDING

A few steps away is King's Theatre, where a troupe performs once or twice daily in the summertime. The plays are always high-spirited comedies — fast-paced for good entertainment.

Additional buildings include a small schoolhouse and the Killeen Cabin of an Irish settler; finally there's the black powder range, where a black powder shoot is held once a year. Such are the real attractions of Kings Landing, because they show what life was like in a St. John River Valley community in the 1800s. At various times, visitors can enjoy lumbermen days, the harvest festival, the Irish, and the Scottish weekends.

FREDERICTON

A BRIEF HISTORY

When Governor Sir Thomas Carleton and his Loyalist supporters moved into the new provincial capital in 1784, they envisaged "a haven for the King's friends" — supported by the Church of England — with a university to prepare their sons for careers in government, the military, or respectable professions such as law and medicine. Land was set aside for the established church, a university, and a military compound, but further progress was slow. It was

not until 1844 that Fredericton was made an Anglican See, but the energetic first bishop, John Medley, completed his handsome stone Gothic-style cathedral in 1853. It was a block from the legislature. King's College, further "up the hill," languished until being reorganized into the nondenominational University of New Brunswick in 1859. Ten years later the British garrison left, but the imperial tradition was kept alive by the local militia, which provided the pomp and ceremony for the annual opening of

the legislature and other staged affairs. When war broke out in 1914 and again in 1939, Fredericton was the site of a basic training centre for the Canadian Army. In the 1950s, Canada's largest peacetime army base — Camp Gagetown — opened in nearby Oromocto, thereby bolstering Fredericton's economy.

For much of the 19th century and well into the 20th, however, Fredericton remained a quiet provincial backwater, its local politicians — many of them Loyalist descendants — seemingly more interested in preserving the status quo than in encouraging commercial growth. They learned little, it seems, from the success of Alexander "Boss" Gibson, who created and ran Marysville, across the river, where his cotton mill was one of Canada's largest in 1885. Two annual events that could not be ignored were the spring log run that filled the St. John River for days, and the arrival of local politicians for what usually was a six or eight-week legislative session. The second event was awaited with some trepidation by the handful of Fredericton-based senior civil servants.

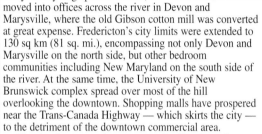

By the mid-1970s, Fredericton had been transformed. The annual log drives were no more (due in part to the Mactaquac Dam 20 km (12 mi.) above the city), and the civil service had become enormous.

Over the next decade, the burgeoning civil service quickly outgrew a new office complex across from the legislature. Besides occupying many nearby large private homes, it moved into offices across the river in Devon and Marysville, where the old Gibson cotton mill was converted at great expense. Fredericton's city limits were extended to 130 sq km (81 sq. mi.), encompassing not only Devon and Marysville on the north side, but other bedroom communities including New Maryland on the south side of the river. At the same time, the University of New Brunswick complex spread over most of the hill overlooking the downtown. Shopping malls have prospered near the Trans-Canada Highway — which skirts the city — to the detriment of the downtown commercial area.

Despite these growth patterns so familiar throughout North America, Fredericton has managed to retain its Loyalist flavour, thanks to a near total absence of industry and the existence of such amenities as Odell Park and the legislature-cathedral focus. It remains a prosperous and refined small town with an almost pastoral lifestyle.

FREDERICTON CITY HALL

A WALKING TOUR

Your walking tour of Fredericton starts at the landmark city hall built in 1876. Here, you can get information about the

city as well as a visitor parking permit that enables you to park free at meters. From here, walk east along Queen Street. On your left, you'll see the military compound, a historic district including the justice building, the N.B. College of Craft and Design, the soldiers' barracks, and the guardhouse before crossing Carleton Street. You may want to view the restored 1827 guardhouse. A 20-minute tour takes you through orderlies' rooms and guards' rooms. The back of the building houses cells for prisoners, first military and later also civilian. Most notable is the "black hole" (literally!) used for solitary confinement. Back on the street, pass the Fredericton National Exhibition Centre (originally the city library), a fine example of Second Empire style, which was fashionable in Fredericton in the 1880s. It now houses temporary exhibits. Farther along Queen Street is Officers' Square. During summer, you can enjoy the hourly spectacle of the changing of the guard, where soldiers in traditional red uniforms march from the nearby guardhouse to Officers' Square and back.

FOUNTAIN AT CITY HALL

OFFICERS' SQUARE

Next to Officers' Square is the York-Sunbury Museum which houses many exhibits on three levels. There's a pioneer kitchen with many tools from a bygone age and a "what'zit" board featuring some of the more exotic implements. You can try your skill guessing what these tools were used for, but if you can't figure it out, the answer is provided. Another display is a grim looking model of a German entrenchment in Flanders during the Great War,

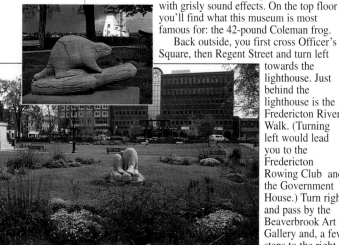

with grisly sound effects. On the top floor you'll find what this museum is most famous for: the 42-pound Coleman frog.

Back outside, you first cross Officer's Square, then Regent Street and turn left towards the lighthouse. Just behind the lighthouse is the Fredericton River Walk. (Turning left would lead you to the Fredericton Rowing Club and the Government House.) Turn right and pass by the Beaverbrook Art Gallery and, a few steps to the right, to the Legislative Assembly Building, an impressive sandstone buiding in Second Empire Style. The Legislative Assembly Building has been the seat of government since 1882. Your guided tour of this elegant building passes along hallways lined with pictures of former lieutenant-governors, into the legislative chamber. Note the cabinet where the mace is displayed. The mace — traditionally a sign of power — is placed next to the table in the chamber whenever the house is in session. In the beautifully decorated chamber, the Speaker of the House sits in the raised chair opposite the door; members of the government sit on the left, the Opposition on the right. Depending on the distribution of the 58 seats, some government members may have to sit next to the Opposition.

YORK-SUNBURY MUSEUM, FREDERICTON

STAIRCASE AT LEGISLATIVE ASSEMBLY

The tour continues by climbing up part of the 12 m (40 ft.) free-standing (and slightly sloping) spiral staircase. Its fancy woodwork includes walnut, cherry, ash, and pine. Upstairs, from the visitors' gallery, you'll get another perspective of the elegant chamber with its huge chandeliers. An adjacent room, used by the Executive Council until it was abolished in 1892, is now used for legislative committees. Back on the ground floor, you may visit the Legislative Library with its collection of New Brunswick and Canadian political

documents. Finally, in the entrance, you can see what may be the finest exhibit — an oversized book with Audubon's color plates of birds from 1820. As the plates would deteriorate under the influence of light, they are kept covered except for viewing.

LEGISLATIVE LIBRARY

Across from the Legislative Assembly Building is the Beaverbrook Art Gallery which houses works by Gainsborough, Dali and an extensive collection of Krieghoff paintings. It also features a variety of travelling exhibitions, some period furniture, and china.

Continue east and pass by the Robert Burns statue. A few steps further east bring you to Christ Church Cathedral, which is not only a National Historic Site but also a well-known landmark. Construction of the massive church began in 1845. The natural stone used for its construction was quarried in New Brunswick, and most of

CHANGING OF THE GUARD, FREDERICTON

STATUE, BEAVERBROOK ART GALLERY

CHRIST CHURCH CATHEDRAL, FREDERICTON

the interior woodwork, such as the wainscot panelling along both sides of the nave, is made of butternut. In the summer of 1911, the cathedral was struck by lightning, suffering severe damage. The many friends of the church made it possible to complete the restoration in about one year's time. The east and west windows are very impressive in their gleaming colours, and there's a distinctive wooden sculpture carved by John Hooper of Hampton, New Brunswick.

From here, we suggest that you walk under the railroad bridge and continue on "the Green" River Walk along the St. John River. You'll pass beautiful homes in various architectural styles. The stately house at 58 Waterloo Row is now residence of the president of the University of New Brunswick. This stately Classic Revival house, built in 1910, has been the home of many prominent people — a judge, a premier, and two lieutenant-governors of New Brunswick. Turn right onto Shore Street and you'll pass by the boyhood home of Fredericton poet Bliss Carman at 83 Shore. Turn right onto University Street. Here, the large Victorian Carriage House, today a bed and breakfast, is an impressive sight. Turn left onto George Street and pass by some beautiful examples of Queen Anne Revival (829 George

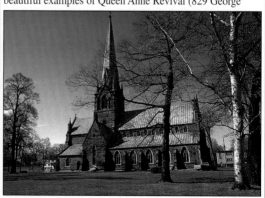

CARRIAGE HOUSE INN

Street) and Gothic Revival (809–811 and 769 George Street). 734 George Street is a Canadian version of a Georgian rectory, built in brick in 1833. Your walk brings you to the Boyce Farmers Market, a must place to visit on Saturday mornings, where you turn right on Regent Street. Follow it to its junction with Queen Street, turn left and return to city hall.

A worthwhile short drive up the hill takes you to the University of New Brunswick.

COTTON MILL FACTORY HOUSES, FREDERICTON

UNIVERSITY OF NEW BRUNSWICK OLD ARTS BUILDING

Its campus is, together with the University of Georgia, the oldest provincial/state university in North America. The Old Arts Building is the oldest Canadian university building still in use.

Another city attraction is the big brick cotton mill and mill town in Fredericton - Marysville, about 10 km (6 mi) from downtown Fredericton. The Government of New Brunswick bought the building for offices in 1985, and in 1986 it was designated a National Historic Site. The rows of plain workers tenements stand next to the Gibson Mill, and the more ornate brick houses on the opposite side of the Nashwaak River illustrate the hierarchy of the mill town. A self-guided walking tour can be found in "A Tour of Boss Gibson's Marysville — a Nineteenth Century Mill Town," available at the York-Sunbury Museum on Queen Street, Fredericton.

OROMOCTO

When General Gage received a land grant in the Saint John River Valley in 1765, he certainly could not have imagined that it would turn into the largest army camp in the Commonwealth. Much of the military history of the Canadian army is preserved at the Military Museum at CFB Gagetown.

The early history of the Canadian Army is very much intertwined with the British Colonial Forces. Beginning with the Boer War in 1899, Canadian regiments were under their own command for the first time. Many of the exhibits go back to that war, in which Canadian Forces joined the British in the fight against the Boers (farmers) — Afrikaners of Dutch descent. These volunteer soldiers arrived at the African shore woefully ill-equipped: the haversacks and helmets were of white canvas, more suited for the snowladen Arctic than Africa; and their "canteens" were just glass bottles. Quite understandably, the soldiers thought the heavy and very fragile one-pint water bottle to be a rather useless thing, especially since the British troops carried aluminum canteens. One day, they were led by Lieutenant Colonel Otter to the Green Point Common. As they passed an old stone warehouse, they took their hated glass bottles out and threw them against the wall. The protest was successful. On arrival at the Green Point Common, they were issued the large felt-covered metal canteens of the British.

After such initial problems, soldiers of the Canadian army distinguished themselves. Of the four Victoria Crosses, Britain's highest award for valour, three were given to Canadian soldiers.

MILITARY MUSEUM, OROMOCTO

You may wonder why the emblem of the Royal Canadian Dragoons includes a springbok. The story is that the Canadian troops were encamped one night when they suddenly realized that the springboks, which had been grazing peacefully in the area, had bolted away at full speed. They realized that the enemy must have spooked them, and so they were warned in time of the "surprise attack." In gratitude to this "reconnaissance unit," the springboks became part of the emblem.

Upstairs you'll see a rifle collection of firearms from 1797 to 1957 that demonstrate the amazing advancement of weapons technology.

You'll notice that one upstairs room is off limits (the entrance is barred), but you can peek in and see the carved furniture and beautiful crystal. This was the mess room, where younger and more senior officers dined together, to get to know each other better and build *esprit de corps*.

GAGETOWN

In the village of Gagetown there are several attractions which make it well worth a stop, as well as a fine country inn (the Steamers Stop Country Inn) and several craft stores and artists' studio.

In town you'll find the Gagetown loomcrafters. As you enter the tiny showroom, you see two loomcrafters working on soft-coloured place mats, table runners, boys' and mens' tartan ties or tartan afghans. Most of the fabrics are made of cotton and wool; a few pieces are woven of linen and acrylic. This isn't mass production. It takes about four days to weave an average afghan. Most of the woven goods are made to order, but the weavers usually make a few extra items, which are sold in the store.

The traditional craft of weaving became popular in Gagetown thanks to the late designer, weaver, and teacher Patricia Jenkins. In 1940, Mrs. Jenkins created the official Royal Canadian Air Force Tartan, and in the 1950s she designed the official New Brunswick tartan.

Today, two people weave in the studio, and four in their own homes. It's a successful small business producing beautiful woven goods that have made a name for themselves. Replicas of garments presented to the Royal Family in the 1950s are on display in the showroom.

LOOMCRAFTERS HOUSE, GAGETOWN

The building that houses the little studio was built in 1761 as a farm outbuilding. About fifty years ago, it was moved to its present location in the peaceful St. John River Valley.

Gagetown's other attraction is the boyhood home of Sir Leonard Tilley, one of Canada's Fathers of Confederation. At the door a costumed guide will welcome you to the 13-room house. Your tour begins in the Loyalist kitchen whose dominating feature is a huge fireplace, built with handmade bricks. There are also two machines that roll thread from a spinning wheel into yarns — a "squirrel cage," and a "weasel." The latter is an innovative design: the turning motion rolls the thread onto a gear with a small pin on the

TILLEY HOUSE, GAGETOWN

side. When the gear completes one revolution (or when a certain length of yarn is rolled), a wooden lever, which is pushed forward by the pin, flaps back with a popping noise — hence the childrens' song "Pop! Goes the Weasel."

Next to the kitchen is the doctor's office. (It was originally the office of Dr. Stickles, who built this house in 1786. Samuel Tilley bought the property in 1818. The medical equipment, however, belonged to the late Dr. Jenkins, father of the famed weaver Patricia Jenkins.) To most visitors the room of the doctor-dentist-pharmacist resembles more a torture chamber than a doctor's office. The folding operating table and the office chair with the clip-on headrest for dental work are vivid examples of what patients had to endure less than a hundred years ago.

In the hallway you will notice a molded "Christian door" whose upper part shows a cross and whose lower part is meant to resemble an open Bible. It is also called a "witches' door," as it was said to keep away bad spirits.

The Tilleys doubled the size of the house by adding two rooms upstairs, as well as a parlour, and a parlour bedroom where Leonard Tilley was born on May 8, 1818.

Ascending the original pine stairs, you reach a cosy children's room with a spool bed, as well as a fancy spruce gum box and a gramophone with cylinder records. Other rooms contain a collection of military memorabilia and fossils and Native artifacts, many of them found along the shores of nearby rivers and lakes. There also are some fine Micmac baskets. The wide wooden floorboards in some of the rooms upstairs were repainted 25 years ago with paint made according to a time-honoured recipe: one plug of tobacco mixed with one pint of ammonia produces the reddish colour you see here. Your travels along the River Valley Scenic Drive end at Saint John. For a description of the port city, see pages 95-107.

FUNDY COASTAL DRIVE

HOPEWELL ROCKS

INTRODUCTION

The key word here is Fundy, for the remarkable body of tidal water that has shaped New Brunswick's southern shoreline. There is nothing quite like the Bay of Fundy anywhere else in the marine world. Its full-moon tides can reach 8.5 m (28 ft.) and during fierce autumn gales they can be even higher. Its many whirlpools and swirling currents act as giant nutrient pumps, bringing in a mixture of tiny marine organisms that in turn lure all manner of creatures, from microscopic cocopods to schools of herring and mackerel, bluefin tuna, and several varieties of whales.

It was this marine activity that first drew humans to Fundy's shores. From the earliest times, aboriginals harvested clam beds and caught herring and salmon in primitive weirs. The first European settlement attempt took place over the winter of 1604–5 when an ill-fated expedition led by Samuel de Champlain encamped on a tiny island in the middle of the St. Croix River.

An unusually severe winter and a resultant scurvy epidemic made the expedition retreat to another Fundy site at Port Royal in what later became Nova Scotia. A generation later, other Frenchmen began trading with

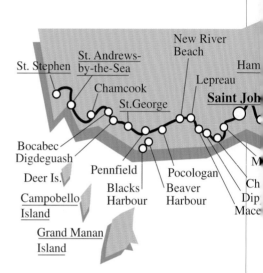

New River Beach

St. Andrews-by-the-Sea

St. Stephen

Ham

Lepreau

Chamcook

St.George

Saint Joh

Bocabec
Digdeguash

Deer Is.

Pennfield

Pocologan

M

Campobello Island

Blacks Harbour

Beaver Harbour

Ch
Dip
Mace

Grand Manan Island

Maliseet groups at the mouth of the St. John River, and there they remained until driven out by the British in the last of the colonial wars in 1763. The site was too good to remain unoccupied, and 20 years later, United Empire Loyalists came ashore to establish Canada's oldest incorporated city, Saint John. Today, it is the commercial pulse of New Brunswick, thanks in part to Fundy's natural advantages.

Much has been made, in story and song, of the Loyalists' influence on New Brunswick — and rightly so. Their arrival created a new colony, which they named New Brunswick; and even though over half of them went back to the United States of America within a generation, the Loyalists left a British tradition — in the government and administrative structures, in the names they gave to many Fundy communities, and in street names. In St. Andrews, for example, all the main streets are named after the 15 legitimate children of George III. The names of the counties — Charlotte, St. John, Kings, Westmorland — were taken from English maps, as were the names of parishes. (This last administrative unit no longer has any function except to define boundaries for political constituencies.)

ST. ANDREWS

Most New Brunswickers remain emotionally attached to their home county. Charlotte's 26,500 residents strongly identify with their county, and with reason, considering their historic ties with Washington County, Maine. Together, they form a truly international community. Most people born in the area have family ties on both sides of the line that stretch back a century or more and are usually linked to the

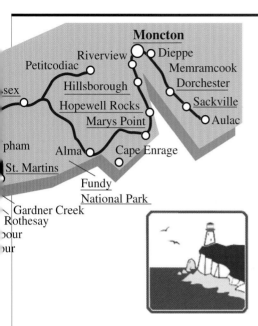

region's forest industry or Fundy's fishery. First the Loyalists and later Irish and Scottish settlers from "the old country" sold their lumber and fish through commercial networks often centred in Boston.

After the devastation of the American Civil War, Charlotte County lumbermen shared in the bonanza of reconstruction. For the next generation, in fact until well into the present century, small coastal schooners made regular trips to and from Boston. Outgoing cargoes of lumber would be exchanged for food, hardware, and invariably, a few kegs of rum. And besides a regular crew, locals would use the vessel as a convenient ferry service.

This tradition of sea trading continues today. Midway between St. Stephen and St. Andrews, tucked into a steep hill out of sight of the highway, is the port of Bayside. A Cuban shipping line makes regular calls, bringing in cargoes of meat and fish and leaving with local products such as seed potatoes and lumber. As well, ships of Greek

**HERRING WEIR,
GRAND MANAN**

HUNTSMAN MARINE CENTRE, ST. ANDREWS

and Russian registry are frequent visitors. Locals can tell when there's a boat in because sailors are often seen walking back from either St. Stephen or St. Andrews, carrying bags of consumer goods unavailable back home.

Another Charlotte County staple is cedar lumber products, which find a ready market in the United States. Two local mills, one overlooking the St. Croix and the other on the outskirts of St. Stephen, keep alive the old Canada–U.S. trade lines. So does the Georgia-Pacific Company complex at Woodland, Maine, which is fed pulp and woodchips harvested from both Charlotte and Washington counties.

Although not so numerous as they once were, herring weirs still give meaning to sustainable fishing by catching small herring that are processed either at Blacks Harbour (at the eastern border of Charlotte) or at Lubec, Maine. As their fathers and grandfathers did before them, today's weir fishermen sell to both sides of the border, although the Connors Bros. Ltd. plant at Blacks Harbour remains the world's largest sardine packer.

The same firm is also heavily involved in a more recent border-spanning venture: salmon cage aquaculture. What began in 1979 as a government-assisted experiment to see whether Atlantic salmon could be reared in cages anchored in the frigid waters of the Bay of Fundy has blossomed into a $100-million a year industry for Charlotte County and as large a business in Washington County. While cage owners in both countries are keen rivals, they share technology and sometimes even brood stock. In fact, the largest operator, Connors Bros. Ltd. has cage sites in both Maine and New Brunswick. And just as the lumber cut in the 19th century along Charlotte County ridges usually found American buyers, so do most of these cage-reared Atlantic salmon.

ALGONQUIN HOTEL, ST. ANDREWS

This international flavour also characterizes Charlotte County's tourist industry. New Brunswick's most famous resort hotel is the Algonquin in St. Andrews. The original structure was built by local businessmen from St. Stephen and St. Andrews but in 1902, two American-born industrialists who rose to fame and fortune in Montreal as head of the Canadian Pacific Railway Company (Sir William Van Horne and Sir Thomas [later Lord] Shaughnessy), bought the facility and created St. Andrews as a tourist town.

Sir William also bought Minister's Island, where he built a luxurious summer "cottage" and an even more impressive barn for his prize Dutch cattle. Sir Thomas stayed closer to the Algonquin in a retreat still called Fort Tipperary. Their presence and international connections were reflected in the Algonquin's clientele, which often included the business and social elite of Montreal, Boston, and New York.

PAINTED TRILLIUM, FUNDY NATIONAL PARK

Today, the Algonquin is owned by the province of New Brunswick but it has kept its CPR connection. The conglomerate's hotel division manages and operates the facility. Minister's Island is also provincially owned and after being closed for years is now open to public tours. Despite its "carriage trade" image, St. Andrews has another prime tourist attraction that is absolutely free — the picturesque wharf with boats coming and going, the spectacular Fundy sunsets, and fish and chips outlet.

The island of Campobello has an even stronger American link than St. Andrews. Physically connected to Lubec, Maine by a modern highway bridge, Campobello is perhaps best known as a summer home for wealthy Americans — most notably American president Franklin Delano Roosevelt. The island's royal grantees, the Owen family, sold most of their property in 1881 to a Boston realty firm. Among those who bought shoreline lots was the Delano family, whose daughter married a Roosevelt. Her son Franklin spent most of his boyhood summers here in a big rambling cottage that has become Campobello's major tourist attraction.

DEER ISLAND WILD ROSES

Another member of Charlotte County's archipelago, Deer Island, has withstood the trend towards summer cottage development. Its quaint villages tucked into sheltered coves were bigger and busier a generation ago when the herring weir fishery was booming. Now Deer Island teenagers must be bused daily to a high school at St. George and many of their parents also commute to mainland jobs. Still, they all remain Deer Islanders and the thriving salmon cage industry is providing more jobs on the island.

The most distant Charlotte County island, Grand Manan, remains first and foremost a fishing community. In contrast to the worldwide trend of vanishing stocks, Grand Manan fishing continues to be good — even great. Proof is the excellent state of local housing and the number of late-model cars, especially the indispensable half-ton.

JETTY, DEER ISLAND

Despite the two-hour ferry ride, Grand Manan has long been a haven for summer residents, both Canadian and American. Since 1945 a number of Fredericton families have fallen in love with Grand Manan, buying and refurbishing old homes and building new ones. Americans have made a major cultural contribution. Buchanan Charles of North Andover, Mass. founded the Grand Manan Historical

Society in 1931 and his remarkable collection of primary material was later donated to the society's archives. Another American summer resident's extensive collection of sea birds is a featured display at the local museum at Seal Cove.

About a half-hour boat ride off Grand Manan is a smaller island. Locals call it Seal Island; Mainers claim it too and know it as Machias but in a typical international compromise, they not only call it Machias/Seal Island but these neighbours have hit on a practical conservation measure. The island's puffin colony has drawn so many birdwatchers over the years that it was decided to limit access. Now a single group of Grand Manan visitors can spend the mornings there, while the afternoon is reserved for a boatload of birders out of Eastport, Maine.

Arriving back on the Fundy mainland at the Black's Harbour ferry terminal, travellers should linger a while, to savour the sights, smells, and sounds of places whose names evoke another age: Back Bay, Mascarene, Beaver Harbour. Wait for low tide to wander along deserted pebbled beaches. Take the road to Lime Kiln Bay and ask anyone on the new ramp if you can see what really goes on at those salmon cages anchored just off shore. Stop at New River Beach Provincial Park for the beautiful scenery and a walk along the rugged Bay of Fundy.

MACHIAS/ SEAL ISLAND

For a unique example of the old and new uses of Fundy resources, turn left at the sign "Point Lepreau" and take a free public tour of what's considered to be the world's most efficient nuclear power generator. Part of the secret to Point Lepreau Power Station's success is the availability of Fundy's cold waters. After the tour, continue on through Maces Bay and Chance Harbour — thriving fishing villages that are home ports for lobster and scallop boats.

Approaching Saint John from the west, stop at Taylor Island for a great view over the Bay of Fundy. There's a public park, with walking trails skirting the Fundy shore and lookout points to view seals and even now and then a porpoise. It's a wonderful picnic stop.

The city of Saint John deserves a long and leisurely visit; after the city you'll be ready for the beaches and other

natural amenities of St. Martins, a former shipbuilding community tucked into a fold of Fundy's shoreline about an hour east of Saint John. That's the last glimpse of Fundy for a spell; there are no roads along this part of the coast, and hopefully there never will be. One part of this magnificent bay should remain in nature's hands.

ATLANTIC PUFFINS

The road from St. Martins to Sussex winds through gentle hill country, passing some of New Brunswick's best and oldest farms. Dairying was introduced about a century ago and it is still this area's economic mainstay. For proof try the ice cream. Not far past Sussex is the turn-off back to the bay and to famous Fundy National Park. The highway through to the main park facilities is as close as you will come to mountainous roads in New Brunswick. Lookout stops just before the road tumbles down to sea level provide a memorable view of the blue waters far below. Fundy is too cold for comfortable swimming, but the park's heated outdoor salt water pool is a wonderful substitute — just one of the park's many attractions. A must-see is Point Wolfe covered bridge, and a few reminders of a once-thriving lumbering mill. It's another great picnic spot.

After enjoying such Fundy gems as the Mary's Point shorebird sanctuary, "the Rocks" whimsically shaped by Fundy's tides, and the many attractions of the bustling city of Moncton, "hang a right at the Dieppe light," as the locals say, and meander along the muddy Petitcodiac, home of the tidal bore, until you find yourself in the heart of old Acadia: Memramcook, and College Bridge — where the University of Moncton had its beginnings. Stay on this former main road, head up the Dorchester Hill — once a challenging grade in the horse and buggy days — and on into the English university town of Sackville, perched on the edge of vast marshes created by the ever-present Fundy tides.

The Bay seems far away now, but the marshes are vivid reminders of its influence. Many have drawn on this natural resource besides the early Acadians who built the original marsh dykes: people as separated in time and perspective as Yorkshire farmers and electrical engineers. The former raised great quantities of marshland hay to feed and fatten their livestock; the latter used the salt content of the marshes to enhance the radio signals that for decades have been spreading the voice of Canada and Canadians through the CBC shortwave station perched on the windswept marsh. All owe a huge debt to the region's most powerful influence, the Bay of Fundy.

ST. STEPHEN

Once a year, in early August, St. Stephen hosts the International Chocolate Festival sponsored and initiated mainly by the Ganong Chocolate Factory. If you want to save the main event of the day for later, you can begin with a visit to the Charlotte County Museum on Milltown Boulevard. It's a short distance away from the town centre and its wide-ranging collection is well worth the effort. The first room represents a street, with old stores along its walls, complete

CHARLOTTE COUNTY MUSEUM, ST. STEPHEN

with antique store signs and products. There is James Ross's cobbler shop, the Vroom Bros. furniture store, and the T. Barry store exhibiting typewriters, lanterns, and similar implements. One distinctive item is a predecessor of today's lottery. It looks like a cribbage board. You pay five cents to play: punch through any hole of your choice, and on the back side, you see what prize you have won. The prizes are mostly Ganong chocolates. In Waterson's drug store you can find primitive hearing aids, jars for leeches (used to stimulate the blood circulation), and moulds for suppositories! A stoneware "pig" — a hot water bottle in the shape of a pig — leads to a display of the regional hospital, with an exhibit of early medical instruments.

Upstairs there's a Chinese collection, a lady's bedroom (featuring a 120-year-old hooked rug with a farm scene), and a kitchen with a massive stove, a daisy churn, and wringers. A music room has artifacts of the Milltown cornet band, another features a lumbering exhibition complete with tools, and there's even a classroom. Not surprisingly, there's a Ganong Chocolate Room, where you can see some of the old chocolate bar moulds, traditional (1909 and 1920) chocolate packages, and some Ganong streetcar signs — "With Ganong Chocolate, no lady can refuse you."

Ganong candy and chocolate production has a long and illustrious tradition here: founded in 1873 by James and Gilbert Ganong, it is Canada's oldest candy manufacturer. One of the world's favourite treats — the chocolate bar — was reputedly created here in 1910; and in the 1930s chocolate-filled heart-shaped boxes, designed for Valentine's Day, captured the market. And kept it! More

chocolates are sold on February 14 than any other day of the year.

You must, of course, see the "sweetheart" of St. Stephen for yourself. Before entering, you exchange your ticket for a white cap, which is compulsory attire inside the plant. The tours are organized like clockwork: every few minutes a group of maybe a dozen enters the building with a guide. You are led through the supply room and past a machine shop to the Lozenges Room with its 19th century machinery. This is the "birthplace" of wintergreen lozenges and double-thick mints. In the next room, candies are dipped into chocolate, a chocolate pattern is sprayed on top, and the shiny round goodies are put in a dryer for about fifteen minutes. They are manually inspected, and if not perfect, sent back. A sweet tip for chocoholics is that the rejects are later dipped again and sold as "double-dips" — cheaper but with almost twice as much chocolate! On to yet another room where a dozen or so large cauldrons are constantly turning — and turning out the ever-popular jelly bean, which is eight days in the making! At the next stop, you can see almond candies being hand-dipped. Last, but certainly not least, you are invited to sample some of the factory's products: everything from chocolate-covered burnt almonds and orange fontant to vanilla frappé, cream toffee, and maple. And then there are the wintergreen lozenges, jelly beans, spearmint leaves, and sour brains. On the way out, you're given a coupon for mint candies, redeemable in the Ganong store in town.

For more information on the Ganong family history consult *The Chocolate Ganongs of St. Stephen, New Brunswick* by David Foster.

While you are in the area, you can enjoy the Crocker Hill Studio and Gardens 2.4 km (1.5 mi.) east of St. Stephen on Ledge Road. Here a beautiful herb and flower garden overlooks the peaceful St. Croix River, with the state of Maine but a stone's throw away.

CHOCOLATE FESTIVAL, ST. STEPHEN

CROCKER HILL STUDIOS, ST. STEPHEN

ST. ANDREWS-BY-THE-SEA

Driving into St. Andrews, from the northeast, N.B. 127 becomes Water Street, the town's main thoroughfare. As the name suggests, it parallels the shore. This is a great place to stroll, to browse around the many stores — from arts and crafts outlets to fine restaurants. You'll find everything here from Wedgewood and Limoges to woodwork made by local craftspeople. All the downtown stores were designed to fit in with the architectural heritage — the gas station, garage, and a supermarket.

St. Andrews' streets follow a grid pattern, with names such as King, Queen, Elizabeth, William, and Princess Royal. Truly, this is Loyalist country! Just a few steps off Water Street is Sheriff Andrews' House on King Street where costumed guides provide tours. Built in 1820, it is an example of a middle-class home of the early 19th century. Little is

ROSS HOUSE AND MUSEUM

known about the owner other than that he had seven children and two servants. A drawing room on the ground floor contains a strongbox — undoubtedly for the sheriff's documents. Three leather fire buckets hang on pegs in the hallway, as required by law. Upstairs, in the master bedroom, there's a wooden bathtub and a corner chair. The third floor, reached by a separate staircase, was the servants quarters. (It's closed off at present.) In the basement-kitchen is a very shallow fireplace,

COURT HOUSE, ST. ANDREWS

specially designed to give off more heat than a deeper one. The current occupants, your guides, bake in the "beehive oven" every day.

Nearby, on the corner of King and Montague Streets, is the Ross Memorial Museum, a neoclassical brick building first occupied in 1824 by the Honorable Harris Hatch. In 1938, Henry Phipps Ross and his wife Sarah Juliette bought the house. He was a minister, and his wife was the daughter of the president of the Bradstreet finance firm, today known as Dun and Bradstreet. Their pictures grace the chandelier-lit

CLAM DIGGING

hallway of the house. Thanks to Sarah's large inheritance, the Rosses travelled widely, returning each year with rare treasures in fine furniture, crystal, and carpets. The "Morning Room" features an 1810 piano. The spacious dining room contains massive mahogany furniture, including two writing desks and a huge bookcase. A spiral staircase leads to the peach and white master bedroom with a round table, masterfully inlaid with mother-of-pearl, soapstone, jade, and other semi-precious stones. Another bedroom features a sleigh bed, and there's a spool bed in the blue guestroom. One room is set aside for exhibits that change annually.

HUNTSMAN MARINE CENTRE, ST. ANDREWS

A short walk away is the impressive County Courthouse and Gaol on the corner of Frederick and Parr Streets. Built in 1840 and now a National Historic Site, it is New Brunswick's best preserved example of a typical mid-19th-century courthouse. The hand-carved Royal Coat of Arms in the pediment was an artistic flourish added in 1858. Continue on Parr Street for seven blocks and then turn right onto Harriet. On the corner of Harriet and Prince of Wales is the huge province-owned Algonquin Hotel, a resort hotel in Tudor Revival style. Return on Harriet Street to the waterfront.

From the town centre, drive on Brandy Cove Road to the Huntsman Marine Science Centre and Aquarium/ Museum. It is named after marine biologist Dr. Huntsman (1883–1973) who stimulated fishery research in the region. One of the attractions is the three harbour seals who are fed twice a day. During the winter they're moved to the aquarium at Shippagan Marine Centre. Displays include a fossilized molar tooth of a woolly mammoth (from the Passamaquoddy Bay), some skulls, and a variety of fish, frogs, and snakes of the area. Useful information is provided on paralytic shellfish poisoning (PSP). The highlight of the centre, especially for young visitors, is the "Touch Pool," where you can actually touch starfish, sand dollars, sea urchins, sea cucumbers, and giant scallops.

SALMON MUSEUM, CHAMCOOK NEAR ST. ANDREWS

If you leave St. Andrews on N.B. 127, you can visit the Atlantic Salmon Centre a few miles out of town. Here, you watch salmon through a large window as they swim, play, and feed. Outside there are two artificial waterfalls, which the salmon leap up from the pool below. At the bottom of the building is the Stream Room with a single window that looks onto the bottom of Chamcook Stream. You can while away the time here watching fish swim by in their natural environment; and they may stop to view the exhibit — you!

CAMPOBELLO ISLAND

Campobello Island remained the feudal fiefdom of a dynasty of Welsh seamen until the late 1800s. Among them was Captain William Owen, who established a settlement there in 1770. The island, connected to the town of Lubec, Maine, by a bridge, gained international recognition in the early 1900s, when it became the "in" place for wealthy Americans who built their summer homes on the island. The most famous such resident was American president Franklin Delano Roosevelt, better known as FDR.

ROOSEVELT COTTAGE, CAMPOBELLO ISLAND

Just beyond the international bridge is the Roosevelt Campobello International Park and Natural Area. A 20-minute film at the visitor centre introduces you to the life of FDR on his "beloved island." Next, you'll see the Roosevelt Cottage, a misnomer if ever there was one, since this stately home has 34 rooms on about 1.62 hectares (4 acres) of land with a fine view of the Bay of Fundy.

FDR's father bought land with an unfinished house in 1883. Two years later, the building was completed and the family moved in for the summer. Just south of that house — today only a marker remains — FDR's mother Sara purchased a cottage furnished in 1910 for a mere $5,000.

This is the red and green building we see today.

The tour of the house also offers a glimpse of Roosevelt the individual. As a little boy all he wanted for Christmas, as he wrote to his mother, was "a box of blocks, and a train, and a little boat." During a summer vacation, in August 1921, Roosevelt developed what was diagnosed as a severe cold after fighting a forest fire, followed by a dip in the icy waters of the bay. A month later, after experiencing partial paralysis, his condition was diagnosed as polio. After that, he only returned a few times to the island. He served as president of the United States from 1933 to 1945.

The house was built as a summer home with no basement, and until 1963 there was no electricity. Your tour is self-guided, but there are guides in some rooms to explain the exhibits. FDR's office (complete with flags) is a good place to start; his small bedroom on the ground floor was situated so as to be easily accessible in his wheelchair. The living room, with wicker furniture, offers an excellent view of the bay. The cottage was later acquired by the oil magnate Armand Hammer, who donated the house in 1963. An international park (jointly administered by Canada and the United States) was established on the property in 1964.

The Hubbards, friends of the Roosevelts, have a summer home nearby. Mr. Hubbard was an insurance broker from Boston. The upper level of Hubbard Cottage is closed to visitors because it's used for conferences. On the ground floor, there's a bright and airy living room furnished in light oak. The dining room is notable not so much for its furniture, but for its unusual oval window and the fantastic view it offers of the bay.

HUBBARD COTTAGE

These "cottages" are by no means the only attractions on Campobello Island. The Roosevelt Campobello International Park and the adjacent Herring Cove Provincial Park both have short hiking trails. From the lighthouse complex at the northern tip of the island — accessible only at low tide — you can enjoy panoramic views.

THE ISLAND OF GRAND MANAN

In the daytime, there is a minor traffic jam on Grand Manan every two hours — when one of the two ferries arrives from the mainland. But once the cars and trucks depart the island returns to its true pace — decidedly leisurely. This approach to life is deeply embedded in its history.

Possibly the island's first visitors were Passamaquoddy Indians collecting eggs of gulls and other seabirds. They

called it mun-a-nouk, meaning Island in the Sea. In 1606, the French explorer Samuel de Champlain was driven ashore on a nearby island. He added the term "Grand" to "Manan," a French corruption of the original Indian name.

Subsequently, the island changed hands a number of times between the French and the English — reflecting the fortunes of war on the faraway continent. In 1784, 50 Loyalist families arrived, and many of today's inhabitants can trace their roots to these settlers. For a time it was unclear whether Britain or the

SWALLOWTAIL PENINSULA

newly independent United States owned the island. The dispute was finally settled in 1842 in favour of the British. Today, most of the 2,500 islanders derive their income from fishing and fish processing, dulse gathering, and tourism.

If you drive south on N.B. 776 you pass Castalia, with its extensive mudflats, a few picnic sites, and the main attraction — the shorebirds. Grand Manan is one of the best places in the entire province to watch birds. About two hundred and fifty species of birds make the island their home. As you enter the village of Grand Harbour, take a sharp left at the corner and drive along the Thoroughfare Road. At the end is a lobster pound, where lobsters are kept in captivity. Ross Island is only a stone's throw away and can be reached on foot at low tide. It is the site of the first permanent settlement on Grand Manan in 1784.

GRAND MANAN LOBSTER POUND

Turn right at Grand Manan Motors and follow the narrow road for 1.6 km (1 mi.). On the right is an unassuming bungalow with some outbuildings which house Rolands Sea Vegetables. The family has been in business for 22 years and warmly welcomes visitors Their mainstay is dulse, a reddish-purple seaweed that is harvested near the shores. Try it, but don't expect it to taste like a vegetable. It's a lot closer to fish, but unique. The dulse is harvested at low tide, then spread out on a net on crushed rock to dry. On a sunny day, it dries in about five hours. The dulse leaves then stick to each other and the harvest can be rolled like a carpet. It first goes into storage, then is ground into flakes or powder. While chewing it seems to be an acquired taste, it is also widely used as seasoning on fish, eggs, and potato salad.

Back on the main road, continue south to the Grand Manan Museum in Grand Harbour. The museum's feature exhibit is a tribute to naturalist Allan Moses (1881–1953), an outstanding taxidermist. The Moses Memorial Bird Collection includes a snowy owl, egrets, wood ducks, mergansers, teals, plovers, killdeer, and falcons. All the birds are well displayed, lighted, and labelled. For more information on bird life and Allan Moses, see L.K. Ingersoll's *Wings over the Sea: The Story of Allan Moses.*

Other exhibits include a large quilt, presented in 1984 by the genealogical society, a 160-year-old loom, and some ancient firearms. The Gannet Marine Exhibition includes information on weir fishing and lobster fishing, which became popular after the lobster trap was invented in 1870. The Gannet Rock Light on display comes from an old lighthouse. In 1904 its kerosene light produced 85,000 candle power and could be seen 20 miles away. An impressive geological exhibit explains the geology of Grand Manan.

DULSE

Continuing further on N.B. 776, you come to Seal Cove. Turn left onto a dirt road opposite the golf course, park somewhere at the end of the road, and climb down the cliffs to the beach. At low tide you can do a bit of exploring, although walking in the soft sand along the beach is laborious. At various points, you will see red and grey rock side by side, the red formation being very old sedimentary rock, the grey, much younger volcanic rock. Whereas the eastern part of the island consists of the old sedimentary rock, the western part is volcanic in origin,

SEAL COVE, GRAND MANAN

GRAND MANAN MUSEUM

and this spot is part of the "fault line," where the two formations join. This is just one of the many places on the island where geologists can study their trade up close.

Back on the main road, continue south, pass the sandy beach at Deep Cove, and stay on the dirt road until the road ends at the Southwest Lighthouse. This part of the island is often shrouded in fog, even when its eastern coast is sunny.

The coastline is very spectacular here with steep, high cliffs. Be careful at the cliff's edge: there are no railings! From the lighthouse, you can walk the 6.1 km (3.8 mi.) trail to Hay Point. As you leave the woods, you descend a fairly steep grassy slope then climb a bit to a promontory, perched high above the sea. The view is fantastic, and there's even a picnic table. If you're lucky, whales may surface, have a blow, and then disappear beneath the waters of the bay.

SWALLOWTAIL LIGHTHOUSE, GRAND MANAN

From the Southwest Lighthouse, you can drive back along N.B. 776 past the ferry terminal to Swallowtail Lighthouse, spectacularly located on a peninsula overlooking the bay. Some herring weirs can be seen far below as well as fishing boats miles off the coast, surrounded by hundreds of gulls. Every two hours, you can see the ferry from the mainland as it rounds the peninsula.

ST. GEORGE

The town of St. George, near Passamaquoddy Bay, is home to about 1,500 people. The houses along the main street are typical Maritime clapboard style. As you drive along Brunswick Street, a big and very substantial looking red and tan building seems to block the way. It's the post office, an impressive structure made of red granite, a building material for which St. George was once famous. To this day, St. George calls itself "Granite Town."

In 1783 the first settlers arrived here from Fort Cumberland, Nova Scotia. One of them was Peter Clinch, a disbanded soldier and native of Northern Ireland, who was given a large land grant between St. George and Letang as a reward for service in the American Revolutionary War. A few steps west of the post office is the Presbyterian Kirk, the oldest Presbyterian church in Canada still in use today. It's a plain white building; inside are box pews typical of churches and meeting halls of the time. Behind the church, not far from the treacherous steep cliffs overlooking the river gorge stands a lonely gravestone amidst the weeds. The scarcely legible inscription says:

PRESBYTERIAN KIRK CHURCH, ST. GEORGE

> By fits and convulsions
> My days were but seven
> Christ died for sinners
> And took me to Heaven.

The infant son of the settlers Moses and Phebe had found peace here in 1805.

A few minutes' walk further on, just in front of a bridge and a visitor centre, is St. George's major attraction — the Magaguadavic Falls and Gorge, pronounced "Machadavic," an Indian word meaning "river of eels." Water plunges from a dam into a deep gorge. A number of smaller falls and rapids are further downstream. A fish ladder allows the salmon to get past the dam on their way upstream to their spawning grounds. The water still foams wildly, but in the

SALMON LADDER, ST. GEORGE

eddies the fish can rest for a while before zigzagging up to the headpond. Some days you can see members of the Atlantic Salmon Federation monitoring the number and health of salmon. They take salmon out just as they make it up the ladder, anaesthetize them, take blood samples, and then put them back in the water.

Conclude your visit by crossing the bridge, turning left onto Campbell Hill, and then left again onto South Street. Here, on the other side of the Magaguadavic River, you have the finest view of the gorge, plus a glimpse of the dam and the red brick generating station of the former St. George Pulp and Paper Co. Turn left again and climb up the hill back to the landmark post office.

Back on highway N.B. 1 at exit 40, drive west for 6.4 km (4 mi.), where you turn left onto Oven Head Road, just behind Ossie's Restaurant. Follow this road for 1.6 km (1 mi.), and you reach Oven Head Salmon Smokers. The salmon processed here are raised at fish farms on Deer Island in the Bay of Fundy. The fish delivered to the smokehouse, average 5 kg (11 lb.), which provides 1.3 kg (3 lb.) fillets. These are dipped in a secret-recipe brine and after they've been dried for about eight hours the smoking process begins. First, small drawers in the smoker are filled with hickory-oak sawdust, which is then lighted. Every so often the sawdust is sprayed with water, so that it keeps smouldering and doesn't start to burn. The temperature is kept below 25° C (80° F). After 30 to 48 hours of this process, the delicacy is ready to be packaged and shipped. If you sample the result you'll immediately know why Oven Head Salmon Smokers products are available not only at the Fredericton Farmers' Market and in some regional outlets, but also at the Atwater Market in Montreal, and in fine restaurants in the United States and even Austria.

THE GORGE, ST. GEORGE

"THREE SISTERS,"
SAINT JOHN

SAINT JOHN

A BRIEF HISTORY

Known as Canada's "most Irish city," Saint John has been
influenced by many other nationalities while maintaining to
the present day its predominantly Irish flavour. The city's
site was once a traditional gathering place for bands of
Maliseets who were probably witness to Samuel de
Champlain's brief stop in 1604 and were nearby during the
Anglo-French imperial wars in the 18th century when Saint
John was a fortified French outpost.

After the French lost possession of Acadia (and Saint
John) the English erected Fort Howe near the homes of
James Simonds and James White, two
Boston merchants who arrived in the
1760s and established Saint John as
the commercial heart of the new
colony of New Brunswick, a role it has
never relinquished. Two years after the
Loyalists landed in 1783, Saint John
became the first city to be incorporated
in British North America.

Over the next generation, Saint John
flourished from the lumbering and
shipbuilding trade, and the most famous
vessel it launched, the *Marco Polo*,
made the city known in the far corners
of the world. After the Napoleonic
wars, waves of Scottish and Irish

FORT HOWE,
SAINT JOHN

immigrants arrived, bringing artisan skills and religious diversity. The Irish potato famine in the 1840s brought thousands of destitute people to Saint John, many of them dying from typhus or the terrible conditions they endured on the passage. Many more died en route. During the spring and summer of 1847, over sixteen thousand passed through the quarantine station at Partridge Island at the harbour's entrance. More than a thousand were buried in mass graves. Most survivors headed for "the Boston States," but some stayed in Saint John and were later joined by relatives and other immigrants.

The decade following New Brunswick's entry into Canadian Confederation was especially difficult for Saint John. It had to cope with new competition from the Intercolonial rail link, which bypassed the port, and in 1877 the entire downtown business area and the docks were destroyed by fire. Undaunted, local leaders convinced the Canadian Pacific Railway to establish a terminus in the port city, but that initiative had little effect upon the steady exodus to the United States.

Like other Maritime centres, Saint John shared in the wartime booms of 1914 and 1939. In 1925 K.C. Irving moved to Saint John to establish a car dealership and went on to build an industrial empire that transformed the province's economy. By 1949, he owned the region's largest bus carrier, all the English-language daily newspapers in Saint John and Moncton, several sawmills, a paper mill, vast forest holdings, Saint John Dry Dock, and an ever-expanding string of service stations selling products from the Irving refinery at Saint John. And his acquisitions continued to grow — all tightly controlled from his Saint John headquarters. By the 1990s, the second and third generation of Irvings were carrying on the family tradition, expanding what was already Canada's largest oil refinery and completing the largest single shipbuilding order — the frigate program — in Canada's history.

TOP: CHAMPLAIN STATUE
ABOVE: TELEPHONE MUSEUM, SAINT JOHN

SHIPYARDS, SAINT JOHN

The city itself began to take on a large image in the 1960s when it incorporated the city of Lancaster and two other parishes. In the 1970s a new highway throughway system and the Harbour Bridge were built; and in the 1980s two mall complexes — including two hotels, an aquatic centre, and a recently added sports complex (Harbour Station) — changed the face of the old downtown area.

Today, a second campus of the University of New Brunswick has developed on a spectacular height of land overlooking Kennebecasis Bay. The regional hospital nearby is the largest single building complex east of Montreal.

A DOWNTOWN WALKING TOUR

Your walking tour of the city begins at Market Slip, by the waterfront. This self-guided walk is an adapted and condensed version of three walks suggested by the city: Prince William Walk, the Loyalist Walk, and the Victorian Walk. For each of these walks, a separate brochure is available at Saint John Visitor Centres.

MARKET SQUARE, SAINT JOHN

The original buildings around Market Square were destroyed by the Great Saint John Fire of 1877. They were replaced by warehouses, some of which were recently incorporated into a distinctive shopping mall.

Beside the landing is Barbour's General Store, an old-fashioned store stocked with period goods, and with a barber shop on the premises. The store was transported here and restored by the Barbour Company Ltd. in 1967 to mark the firm's 100th anniversary. In its heyday, this general store had everything one would need, from fabrics to food. The barber shop advertises a ten-cent shave — a reminder of times past.

Turn right onto Prince William Street whose historic brick buildings have an old-city feel. At the corner of Princess Street, on your right, is Chubb's Corner, formerly the stock exchange. High on the building's facade, stone faces look down onto the street: some are grim, some laugh, seemingly with malice. When carved by a local artist, they prompted angry newspaper comments: "We trust no more of our buildings will be adorned by such buffoonery from his hands." Across the street is Old City Hall,

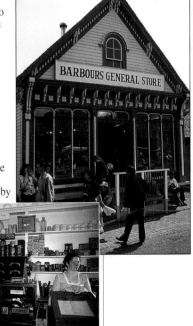

constructed in 1878. On the right is the massive Bank of New Brunswick with its fluted columns. This was Canada's first chartered bank. At 154 Prince William is the Seamen's Mission, founded by Lady Tilley, wife of Sir Leonard Tilley, one of the Fathers of Confederation. Passing the Saint John High School, you reach three residences at 262–268 Prince William, perched high above the street and the harbour. Their suburban style constrasts starkly with the urban houses you passed earlier. A few steps ahead is The Three Sisters, a street lamp that helped guide sailors into the harbour — a white light to the land side and a red light towards the sea.

BELOW: ORANGE STREET
BOTTOM: MECKLENBURG STREET, SAINT JOHN

Walk up one block of St. James Street, turn left on Canterbury, and then right again on Queen Street. Crossing Germain Street, you'll see a number of Second Empire-style townhouses including the former home of Sir Leonard Tilley. Continue to Queen's Square, an inviting place to stop amidst shady trees, next to a statue of Samuel de Champlain, who named the town more than 300 years ago. (Note that the walkways across the park form a Union Jack.) From its centre, cross the park at an angle, keeping to the left. A few steps further left bring you to Mecklenburg Street, named after Charlotte of Mecklenburg-Strelitz, a German fiefdom. She was the consort of King George III at the time of the Loyalists' arrival in Saint John. On the corner of Sydney and Mecklenburg is Caverhill Hall, an imposing stone building. It was built by Simeon Jones, brewer and mayor of Saint John. It is a copy of a building Jones had seen in Montreal. Continue on Mecklenburg Street to its junction with Carmarthen, and then turn left.

Walk two blocks and turn right onto Orange. This short stretch is one of the most architecturally interesting parts of the walk. The properties are well kept, and show a variety of style. Numbers 70 and 78 Orange Street were the homes of prominent Saint

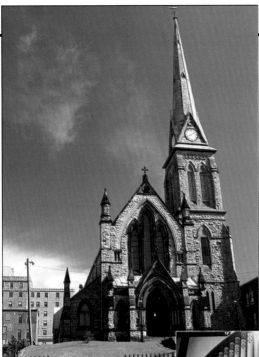

TRINITY CHURCH,
SAINT JOHN

John businessmen. At 71 Orange Street was an impressive sandstone edifice built by George MacLeod for his shipping and lumber business. Mr. MacLeod originally lived at number 79, one of three Italianate houses on the corner of Orange and Wentworth. The stone carvings around the doorways are worth noting. Turning left on Wentworth for a block, walk to the corner of Wentworth and Princess Streets. Number 99 is a pretty Second Empire-style house. Nearby, you can see part of the Saint John Harbour.

A few steps away is the very imposing Centenary-Queen's Square United Church. The original Centenary Methodist church built here in 1839 was a monument to a hundred years of Methodism. It was destroyed in the Great Fire of 1877, and the present gothic structure was built on the site in 1882. When Centenary Methodist and Queen's Square United churches merged in the 1950s, the new name was adopted. The fine interior has 13 stained glass windows. The most prominent, the Great South Window, is 6 m (20 ft.) wide and 12 m (40 ft.) high.

SAINT JOHN
TOWNHOUSES

From the church, turn left onto Princess Street and follow it to its intersection with Sydney. Across the street on the right is the Parkerhouse Inn, one of New Brunswick's heritage inns. It was constructed in 1891 by Dr. W. White, surgeon and twice mayor of Saint John. Continue along Princess to Germain, where you turn right. A few

KING'S SQUARE,
SAINT JOHN

steps brings you to Trinity Church. First built in 1788, it was destroyed in the Great Fire of 1877. It was rebuilt in 1879 on the same site. The Royal Coat of Arms, which survived the fire, is mounted over the west door.

Exit the church through the back door and you'll find yourself back on Charlotte Street. Turn left and walk to King's Square, the counterpart to Queen's Square, with walkways in the shape of the Union Jack. It's a favourite resting place for foot-weary shoppers, children, musicians, and a multitude of pigeons.

On Sydney Street, right next to the Old County Courthouse, is the new Saint John Firefighters' Museum. Inside, right next to the entrance is an old hand pumper, a wagon with two long handles on its sides. Six volunteers were stationed at each handle; they pulled down alternately, thus operating two pistons that pumped the water through two hoses. The era of the hand pump (from 1786 to 1863), was the first phase in mechanized firefighting. The next development, the horsedrawn steam engine, lasted until the beginning of the Great War in 1914. Then came the motor car, and everything changed. Upstairs is a red alarm box once seen all over town. This

EXHIBITS AT THE
FIREFIGHTERS'
MUSEUM, SAINT
JOHN

one still works and you are even invited to pull the lever. This sets off the alarm, and ticker tape comes out at the station with punched-in numbers that identify where the alarm originated. There are many other artifacts, as well as

pictures showing the utter devastation of the Great Fire, that destroyed two-thirds of the city.

SAINT JOHN MARKET

From the museum, walk around King's Square counterclockwise to Charlotte Street. Cross the street and enter the Old City Market. The produce ranges from fresh apples to dulse, beans, lobster, and freshly baked muffins. Few can leave the market empty-handed. The interior shape of the building is rather unusual — it resembles the inverted hull of a boat, an appropriate symbol in a city made rich by shipbuilding. The design of the building was the result of a competition among local architects.

Just opposite the market enter a large shopping centre (One Brunswick Square), and take the escalators to the second floor to the NBTel and Telephone Pioneers Museum. Here, a volunteer will explain the history of the telephone over the last 120 years. People were slow to adopt the new device. The first Saint John directory of subscribers is one page long! In 1909 the first coin phones were introduced, at five cents a call, and in 1928 Saint Johners got their first dial phone. The first switchboards had one supervisor assigned to every five or six women. She was issued a stick, which she used to insure that orders were followed and no private calls were made! By 1952 there were 50,000 telephone connections in New Brunswick. In the 1980s fibre optics replaced wires. The new technology allows 3,600 calls to be sent through a single strand.

TELEPHONE MUSEUM

Nearby, on the corner of Union and Germain Streets, is Loyalist House — the oldest restored house in Saint John and one of the oldest in New Brunswick. Both outside and in, it's a study in design and the customs of the day. The beautiful doors in the hallway are curved, which required careful steaming of the wood. There is a Bible on the sewing table in the living room. Sunday was supposed to be a day of rest, but

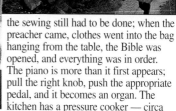

LOYALIST HOUSE, SAINT JOHN

the sewing still had to be done; when the preacher came, clothes went into the bag hanging from the table, the Bible was opened, and everything was in order. The piano is more than it first appears; pull the right knob, push the appropriate pedal, and it becomes an organ. The kitchen has a pressure cooker — circa 1795! Another deceptive item is the commode of bird's-eye maple. It has a decorative façade of false drawers. The entire top folds back, and there's the chamberpot.

Back on the street, continue up Wellington Row to the Saint John Jewish Historical Museum. It contains a small schoolroom, where children study the Hebrew language and customs two afternoons a week. There's a small chapel, where the congregation still worships during the winter, when it is uneconomical to heat the large synagogue. In the basement are some photographs of Mr. and Mrs. Solomon Hart, the first Jews to arrive in Saint John, in 1858. The city's first synagogue was built in 1898.

SYNAGOGUE, SAINT JOHN

Many immigrants arrived from Eastern Europe in the early years of this century. Between 1920 and 1960, up to three hundred Jewish families lived in Saint John, but their numbers have decreased substantially in recent years.

One room is devoted to the Mikvah, a religious purification bath. It is used by women after childbirth, men before Rosh Hashanah, the Jewish New Year, and at other occasions. Another room contains a variety of artifacts such as children's scrolls and figurines from the Middle East. Two other rooms change themes annually to show aspects of Jewish community life in Saint John. A volunteer guide will take you around the corner to the large synagogue, which was erected in 1870 as a Calvinist church. The massive arcs with their beautiful wood carvings are an imposing feature.

STONE CHURCH,
SAINT JOHN

Just across from the synagogue is the St. John's Stone Church, built in 1824. Its stained glass windows were imported from England, Germany, and Toronto. The kneelers were made by 14 women of the congregation in the 1950s, and it took them two years to finish the task. Upstairs are the original pews. One stone in the altar stands out conspicuously. It is from a church in Steyning, Sussex, England, built between 1047 and 1066 and destroyed during the Second World War. It has been put in the same place in this church that it occupied in the older one. Outside, high up on the tower, are 32 gargoyles whose faces probably represent the builders of the church.

From here, retrace your steps to King Street, Saint John's major downtown artery, from where you return to Market Slip.

MARTELLO TOWER,
SAINT JOHN

OTHER SAINT JOHN ATTRACTIONS

The Carleton Martello Tower rises prominently on a rocky knoll. It was begun as a fortification in the war of 1812, but by the time it was finished, the war had ended. The tower has four floors. The interior of the circular structure (named after Cape Mortella on the island of Corsica) consists of a single room with a large supporting pillar in the centre. Along the brick walls are the bedsteads of the soldiers, complete with folding cot, mattress, pegs for their scarlet uniforms, canteens, and firearms. The basement is a heavily constructed powder storeroom. To reduce the risk of explosions, the only source of light was a single lantern. Upstairs you can see a short video and get a fine view across the city.

Opposite the Irving Pulp and Paper Mill is Reversing Falls, one of the most famous attractions in Saint John. However, you may not see anything extraordinary happen here if you don't

know what to look for. A visitor information centre, complete
with video presentations and viewpoints, is located on a steep
cliff overlooking the St. John River near its mouth.

If you arrive when the tide is going out, you'll see the
river doing what it is supposed to do — flowing
downstream to empty into the Bay of Fundy. It does so
quite vigorously; there are pools and eddies, and it is not
safe for boats to run the rapids. After about six hours, the
tide starts to come in again, and the water in the bay rises.

At some point, the pressure of the river's water flowing
down and the water of the bay pushing up is equal. This is
low slack tide, and now it is safe for boats to pass through
— but only for twenty minutes. After that, the water of the
bay rises so much that it actually pushes the water up the
river. For about six hours, the water flows upstream. When
the water in the bay stops rising, there is a standstill: high
slack tide. Again, for a short time, boats can pass safely
through the narrows. Then the water starts flowing
downstream again, and the cycle is repeated.

The best way to view this phenomenon is to enquire
about the current tide status, and to watch the process twice
— once as the water flows upstream and again as it flows
downstream. Good viewpoints are located on top of the
visitor centre and at a point opposite the Irving Pulp and
Paper Mill. The latter is reached by passing the visitor
centre, turning left onto Douglas Street, and left again,
following the sign. At this point, there are two small islands
in the river, and the water flowing past them, foaming and
frothing, creates a spectacular sight.

The New Brunswick Museum is housed in an impressive building on Douglas Avenue — a street lined with many historic houses. Its displays range from a Chinese collection to ship artifacts, including navigational instruments. The MacIntosh Gallery of Natural History, on the second floor, depicts 300 years of New Brunswick's history and is notable for its outstanding collection of Loyalist artifacts. There is also an impressive exhibit of huge bones of sperm whales taken from the Bay of Fundy. Mounted foxes, wolves, and cougars are exhibited together with New Brunswick reptiles, such as the common snapping turtle. Trilobites from the so-called Saint John Group are believed to be 590 million years old. The display includes the teeth and bones of a mastodon, an elephant-like creature that roamed New Brunswick's forests during the last ice age.

Historical Fort Howe lookout is perched high above the city. Constructed in 1777 in Halifax, the fort was later disassembled and re-erected at Saint John to protect the harbour from American privateers and hostile Indians. Within one year, all raids had stopped, and from 1785 on the blockhouse served as the first jail of the newly incorporated city of Saint John. Today, the small fort is locked and there is little to see at the blockhouse itself. The main attraction is the location, and the panoramic view of the city.

LOYALIST DAYS

The narrow bay at the market slip is filled with people, young and old. Two boats come into view, propelled by a number of young men at the oars. The boats carry the King's Loyals in period costumes. Just before they reach the pier, the long oars are raised, and the boat is pulled ashore. The Loyalists have landed.

From here, the entourage climbs up the pier and heads down to the temporary open-air auditorium in front of Barbour's General Store. At this point, the mayor officially opens the Loyalist Days celebrations, the National Anthem is

LOYALIST DAYS, SAINT JOHN

sung, and a prayer is spoken. The week-long festival is underway.

This annual re-enactment marks the anniversary of the landing of a fleet of more than two thousand Loyalists who arrived at the mouth of the St. John River, from May 10–18, 1783. They had fled their homes in the thirteen colonies at the end of the Revolutionary War, fearing persecution for their loyalty to the crown. The first arrivals were mostly civilians from all walks of life. They were followed by a second fleet in June and a third in September, carrying Loyalist troops. In addition, numerous individual vessels of all kinds arrived here. Few of the settlers were prepared for living in the wilderness, and many had to stay in tents and makeshift huts through the first winter. They established two settlements that later became Saint John.

Two other events at the Loyalist Days are worth mentioning. One is the military encampment, which is set up in front of Barnhill School on Manawagonish Road. Most of the heavy canvas tents are small A-frame affairs without floors; straw is used as mattresses. This living exhibit gives a good impression of the day-to-day life of Loyalist servicemen and their families.

Whereas the military encampment is shown throughout the week, the military re-enactment takes place only during certain days of the festival. For about an hour, a small contingent of infantry and artillery demonstrate their skills. At King's Square in the city centre, soldiers march to the beat of a solitary drum, fire their muskets, and at times even charge at the invisible enemy with their bayonets. In another corner, artillery soldiers fire a small cannon, drowning out the shots of the pistols in the general din. After an hour, the cannon and muskets are quiet, the drum is put to rest, and the ubiquitous pigeons are back, eagerly picking up chips and fries.

The Loyalist Days Festival takes place each year for a full week in mid-July. There are all sorts of entertainments, such as demonstrations by the Coast Guard, a parade, and concerts on King's Square. For details, call Loyalist Days Inc. at 634-8123.

PARTRIDGE ISLAND

When the Loyalists first landed on May 10, 1783, they set foot not on the mainland, but on a tiny island less than a mile away from the port of Saint John. The place is called Partridge Island, and over the years it became the Canadian equivalent of Ellis Island off New York City. From 1785 to 1942, three million immigrants landed here, many from Eastern Europe.

About half of them moved on to the United States; of those who stayed in Canada, some settled in New Brunswick, but most moved west. Their first impression must have been a wet and smelly one: they were first deloused with a kerosene shower, followed by a hot-water shower to take away the oily smell. In the meantime their belongings were steam-cleaned.

If you want to find out more about these immigrants, their plight, suffering, and survival, Partridge Island is the

PARTRIDGE ISLAND

place to visit. Currently, tours to the island leave from the wharf at the market slip. The short boat ride provides views of the harbour and skyline of Saint John, the Carleton Martello Tower, and often a few seals. As you land on the island, a sign says "Passports please." This is where you hand over your ticket, which looks like a Canadian passport — symbol for the entry into the new country. As you climb the hill towards the museum and the lighthouse, you'll see crumbled foundations of buildings. They are the remains of the many hospitals on Partridge Island.

A visit to the small museum, which displays pictures of immigrants from many countries, confirms the grim initial view: immigration in these days was definitely not fun and games. Two thousand Irish immigrants died here of typhus fever. They were treated by the dedicated young physician Dr. Patrick Collins, who himself fell victim to the disease. A biography of Dr. Collins has been written by Harold E. Wright, entitled *James P. Collins, MD*. Another exhibit depicts the landing of Danish immigrants in the 1870s.

Back outside, the sparkling red-and-white lighthouse, is a contrast to these reminders of a difficult past. Nearby is a bunker with subterranean rooms for men and ammunition — a memento of the Second World War, when a German attack was expected. It never came. Next to the bunkers is a majestic Celtic cross erected to commemorate the fever victims and the dedication of Dr. Patrick Collins.

Down near the beach is a small grassy area, neatly fenced in. This is a graveyard, partitioned into three parts: one for Protestants, one for Catholics, and one for Jews. In this quiet place you can muse on the history of the region.

ST. MARTINS

ST. MARTINS

Approaching St. Martins from Saint John on N.B. 111 leads you through hilly, pastoral landscape with hamlets, fields, and woods. As you turn into the town of St. Martins, it seems that you have entered another world, no longer rural, but not quite a resort. Charming, maybe. Quaint, surely. Well-kept houses line both sides of the road, a number of bed and breakfast places, and Victorian homes converted to inns. Just beyond the fine St. Martins Country Inn on the left, the road climbs, and at its high point there's a fantastic view across Quaco Bay, Old Pejepscot Wharf, the bicentennial lighthouse, and two covered bridges. At low tide, the boats are high and dry on the shore along the wharf. Lobster traps are stacked up in four or five layers. If you turn right, you pass through one of the covered bridges, and continue to Mac's Beach.

The Cave View Restaurant sits alone on the beach; at high tide, the water reaches almost to its doors, but at low tide, you can walk along the pebble beach. The "pebbles" are big, so it's slow going. If you keep to the left towards a rocky outcrop, you are stopped by a gurgling creek. On the other side, at the foot of the cliffs, are the sea caves, not caves really, but wide cavities in the rock that will be filled with water come high tide. If you round the corner of the cliffs you can explore the shoreline further. When the tide comes in, you can sit around in a cozy inn somewhere in town. St. Martins offers a slower, more relaxed way of life.

HAMPTON

Kings County Museum in Hampton is housed in two rooms on the ground floor. It features a collection of local artifacts along with uniforms, and a number of pictures including a portrait of King George V, called "A Quiet Smoke."

From here, a guide will take you to the adjacent jail where you can get a feel for prison life in the 1800s. The building has not always been at this site. In 1871 the 64-year-old prison was totally dismantled, its individual pieces were towed by oxen and horses across snow and ice from Kingston to Hampton, where the building was reassembled for continued use as a jail. The thick-walled cells on the ground floor are only about 1.8 x 3 m (6 ft. x 10 ft.). A small chamberpot sits in the far corner.

One of the jail's most memorable inmates was a horse thief and escape artist Henry More Smith (a.k.a. Henry Frederick Moon, a.k.a. William Newman). According to Sheriff Bates, who had arrested him several times, Smith faked illness so well that he fooled the doctor in attendance. Supposedly dying, he jumped from his deathbed and was not recaptured for two months. Back in jail, Smith broke the iron chains and removed the iron collar riveted around his neck. After being sentenced to death, he faked insanity by performing in his cell a puppet show with handmade marionettes. People were amazed that he had made the puppets with only straw from his bed and cloth from his shirts. Furthermore, he had made them while handcuffed and chained to the floor of his cell by heavy ox-chains! Small wonder that,

some people thought he was helped by evil spirits. For those interested in mystery and stories about law enforcement of old, we recommend *The Mysterious Stranger* by Walter Bates and *Lunar Rogue* by Barbara Grantmyre, both dealing with horsethief Henry More Smith.

Today, other cells on the ground floor and upstairs house exhibits of a country kitchen, a bedroom with a bed featuring an interesting tree-like headboard, a classroom with books from that period, and many other items. The upstairs cells, have small openings in the inside walls — the only place where the prisoners had contact with the outside world. Through these holes they received their food from the guards.

If you want to see some of the architectural heritage of Hampton, walk from the parking lot onto Centennial Drive, turn left, make a right and stroll around the block. There are a number of beautiful old private homes along the way.

SUSSEX

"Twenty-five-and-a-five-and-a-five-and-a-five, nobody interested for twenty-five? ... Last call, and sold for twenty-three," sings out Alvin Buchanan, the auctioneer at the Co-op Cattle Sale in Sussex. Sussex is the dairy centre of New Brunswick, and as long as there is livestock, Sussex

AGRICULTURAL MUSEUM, SUSSEX

will have cattle sales by auction. They began 1841, but the first co-op sale took place in 1957. It has become a tradition here every Wednesday morning, and they haven't missed a single Wednesday yet as the auctioneer proudly recounts. If you're in town on auction day, be sure to stop by. The setting is decidedly rural; middle-aged men with ballcaps dominate the scene. And they are not here for the thrill of the auction, but for business. Long before the auction begins, they have inspected the cattle, each marked with an identifying number. Holstein and Jersey calves, goats, and porkers — just about everything with four legs is sold here. This is almost a family affair, with the auctioneer knowing most of his customers by name. Thus, there is no need for numbers, or many of the other formalities required at the more anonymous city auctions. Still, tourists are definitely welcome to this lively event.

Your next stop in Sussex could be the New Brunswick Agricultural Museum. It opened its doors in 1986, and new exhibits have been coming in ever since. Your tour starts in a big room with an assortment of sleds, some for hauling groceries from town, others for enjoyment. A buffalo robe kept the legs of the passengers warm on cold winter trips. A huge threshing machine, the "Little Giant," was actually

CATTLE AUCTION, SUSSEX

made right here in Sussex. The large, black shawls on the wall are nets to keep the flies away from the horses when they drew a hearse.

And then there are the theme rooms: a typical rural kitchen, a small bedroom, a living room, and a school room with slate boards and double wooden desks. Another room is dedicated to tools — everything from log hooks, adzes, and a surveyor's chain for measuring distances, to one of the first milking machines. There is an early pushable potato crop duster, a milk tester, a froe for making shingles, and a shaving horse. From here, your guide takes you to the adjacent blacksmith shop, with its collection of oil lamps, the forge, and portable blacksmith equipment. The latter was particularly useful as most farms were located far apart and it was a lot easier if the blacksmith took his services to his customers. Your tour ends at an old train station where circular black markings on the original hardwood floors remind you where the milk cans stood. It was by train that farmers got their products to the markets. The caboose next to the station is one of the last of a dying breed, a relic of the recent past: within the last few years, it has been replaced by an electronic black box.

PETITCODIAC

If you have a special place in your heart for dolls, you might want to take a short detour off the Fundy Coastal Drive to the town of Petitcodiac where you'll find a special doll museum. In 1987, owner Lena Clarke bought an old warehouse from the CP railroad company, had it moved and completely remodelled for her purpose. Her initial collection consisted of just a few dolls of her own and her daughters. Soon, however, the collection started to grow and she received dolls from all over the world from friends and family. At present, there are about 4,000 dolls in the museum.

Upon entering the museum, you soon become aware of the variety of dolls displayed here, ranging from the popular to the unusual, from the simple to the refined. Smurfs and Pillsury Doughboy along with the likenesses of Cher and the Osmonds are some of the simple, modern, dolls that contrast starkly with handcrafted dolls depicting members of the Royal Family, and a Hopi Khachina from Northern Arizona. Spanish dolls with elaborate dresses are displayed along with Russian stacking dolls. Of specific interest is a Peruvian doll scene showing a woman in labor assisted by three midwives and "Fundy Folk Dolls", showing a 19th century fisherman and his wife of the nearby Fundy Coast.

FUNDY NATIONAL PARK

Imagine walking beneath tall, stately maple trees on a well-groomed trail, passing a beaver pond, then up a hill to a viewpoint overlooking a bay that boasts the highest tides in the world. That, and much more, is Fundy National Park. Here are 206 km² (80 sq.mi.) of heavily wooded terrain, laced with 100 km (60 mi.) of hiking trails. Early settlers once made their homes along the bay to take advantage of the fertile land. The highest point is about 365 m (1,200 ft.),

UPPER SALMON RIVER

BENNETT LAKE

high enough to have a variety of ecosystems: from the softwood-clad windswept cliffs along the bay to large stands of beautiful hardwoods; from boggy swamps reminiscent of the ice age to deep river gorges with roaring waterfalls. More about the geological, natural, and human history is described in Michael Burzynskis' *Fundy National Park*.

Founded in 1950, the park offers activities as diverse as camping, hiking, boating, birdwatching, lawn bowling, and swimming. There is also a nine-hole golf course, complete

MATTHEW'S HEAD

with some of the resident deer that frequently show up to watch the game, and be seen. There are frequent guided nature walks and talks.

One of the park's attractions are the two covered bridges. These used to be a common sight in New Brunswick, but their numbers are diminishing quickly. In 1990, the Point Wolfe Bridge in Fundy National Park was accidentally destroyed by a work crew while blasting. Fortunately, it was replaced, thus preserving if not the original heritage, at least the look and feel of it.

The park has its own newsletter, *Salt & Fir*, which is free at all visitor centres. It describes events and activities in the park and its surroundings.

In addition to a motel, chalets, and literally hundreds of drive-in campsites, there are 14 wilderness campsites awaiting backpackers who want to "get away from it all."

MARY'S POINT

Mary's Point is known far and wide as a place where you can enjoy spectacular views of migrating birds at the right time of the year. A narrow footpath slopes down past a small museum where you can get information on bird migration and various species. Further down, there's a platform for watching the birds, but the best vantage point is at the beach, where large tree trunks indicate the end of the trail. Walking any further would mean disturbing the roosting birds.

Thousands of sandpipers and plovers of various subspecies congregate here on the mudflats after the tide goes out. They feed on tiny mud shrimps and worms. In mid-August, well fed and rested, the birds are ready for the 60-to-90-hour flight to their winter quarters in northern South America. Among the birds roosting on the beach resembling pebbles of gravel on the sand, is the semipalmated plover, a chubby little bird with a single black band across its white breast. Its flying and roosting companions are the fairly large, orange-legged ruddy turnstone and the semipalmated sandpiper.

One minute the flock roosts and another, amidst a sudden wave of flashing dark and silvery light a dense clump of birds arcs swiftly into the air along the shore, shifting this way and that way in a graceful manner. Then they settle down on the beach and repeat their spectacular performance a little while later. It is an amazing mystery, how they can fly so fast and so close together without bumping into each other. Another important migratory site is located across the Shepody Bay at Dorchester Cape. Mary's Point, however, is more spectacular for the viewers.

SANDPIPERS, MARY'S POINT

HOPEWELL ROCKS

If you park just inside the gate and walk to the viewpoint next to the restaurant, you may see nothing but a few very small islands known as "The Rocks." A steep iron staircase leads down to the water. What is it about this place that makes people come back time and again?

HOPEWELL ROCKS

At high tide, the Rocks aren't very impressive, but when the tide falls, the fascination of the place immediately becomes apparent. Pick up a tide schedule at the little information building and plan to come back at low tide. Then you can walk down the three flights of iron stairs and stroll on the ocean floor, around the base of the "little islands," now towering towards the sky.

BARNACLES

Some of the ocean floor is soft, wet sand, some mud, and some rock. The reef you walk on looks brittle, but it is a surprisingly solid conglomerate rock. The exposed surface is blanketed with barnacles — little volcano-shaped shells. Next to them you'll find rockweed, a curious seaweed with small oval bladders at its tips.

What are the forces responsible for this first-rate natural wonder? About twice each month, when sun, moon and earth are positioned on one line, the gravitational forces of sun and moon add up, and tides are about 20 percent higher than normal. This is called spring tide, referring not to the season, but an old English/Germanic word springan, or "to jump." On the other hand, when sun, moon, and earth form a right-angled triangle with earth at the vertex of the 90 degree angle, the gravitational forces subtract and tides are lower than normal, a

HOPEWELL ROCKS

phenomenon called neap tide. These tidal effects are the same all over the world, but here in Fundy Bay, they are much more visible than elsewhere. This is due to the length and shape of the bay, which acts as a funnel, pushing the water inward. As there is no exit, the water level rises dramatically. The average change in water level at the Rocks is 10.7 m (35 ft.). The largest change ever measured there was 14.8 m (48.6 ft.). In other words, the water rises and falls the height of a four-storey building.

Upon returning to the stairs, you may choose to continue walking along the coast rather than ascending the staircase. The cliffs gradually get lower and less impressive, until, after a short distance, you reach a very wide, gently sloping beach. Here, a boardwalk takes you back to the parking lot.

ALBERT COUNTY MUSEUM

Your self-guided tour begins on the ground floor of the museum. At the back of the building are three cells of the former jail with massive 26-inch walls, and three-inch iron bars on the windows. Particularly chilling is the dungeon

ALBERT COUNTY MUSEUM

— a cell used for solitary confinement with a big iron ring in the centre to which unruly prisoners in leg irons were anchored. Notice the axe mark in the wooden door. It played a part in one of the most famous murder trials in the county, the so-called "Rectory Murder," details of which are described in the displays. In December 1906, the housekeeper of the parish priest was brutally murdered in the course of an attempted robbery, while the priest was out of town. Evidence seemed to point to Tom Collins, a young man who had come from Ireland only months before. He had worked as handyman around the rectory in New Ireland, a hamlet no longer in existence, but

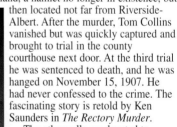

then located not far from Riverside-Albert. After the murder, Tom Collins vanished but was quickly captured and brought to trial in the county courthouse next door. At the third trial he was sentenced to death, and he was hanged on November 15, 1907. He had never confessed to the crime. The fascinating story is retold by Ken Saunders in *The Rectory Murder*.

The other cells are devoted to historical photo displays. There are pictures — with explanatory text — of the Stoney Creek Oilfields, which went into production in 1913 and continued for 30 years. Albertite, a mineral unique to this area, was discovered in 1820. It is essentially congealed petroleum. Other photo displays deal with sawmills, shipbuilding, and covered bridges. Upstairs, is a photo display of various architectural styles

ALBERT COUNTY
MUSEUM

in Albert County. There are also some unique artifacts such as an inkwell made from the hind hoof of a large moose, and hand-carved thorny picture frames.

Outside the museum is the forge. The fireplace with its large bellows was common in shops of the period.

The adjacent large barn contains a lot of farm equipment, including a stump harrow, horse tread, and butter churns. One of the more unusual items is a dog tread, which used dogs as a power source. There's also a complete pioneer kitchen.

Walk across the picnic site to the stately courthouse, built in 1904, to replace the original (1846), which burned down in 1902. The predominant style is Classic Revival, and its most unusual feature is the ceiling decoration of pressed tin. The courtroom contains a prisoner dock, witness stand, raised seating area, and a public gallery.

PIONEER KITCHEN,
ALBERT COUNTY
MUSEUM

HILLSBOROUGH

Here is a great chance to return to the days before cars and planes — when trains were the preferred means of travel. New Brunswick's only operating historical train is permanently stationed at Hillsborough. From here you can take an old-fashioned one- or three-hour outing in a 1914 railroad car trimmed with the luxurious wood panelling. As you ride towards Salem, the fields slowly change to marshes where you may see brilliantly coloured pheasants and then to woods. All the while the engine, which dates back to 1899, is huffing and puffing, climbing out of the valley to higher terrain and across a trestle bridge. Longer dinner excursions take you all the way to Baltimore Station where Dobson hiking trail (from Moncton-Riverview to Fundy National Park) crosses the tracks.

At the station, you can marvel at several old railroad cars, one used for a museum display and gift shop. The large building at the end of the tracks used to be a gypsum mill. Today, it houses more railroad cars and locomotives as well as repair facilities where equipment is restored.

STEEVES HOUSE,
HILLSBOROUGH

Hillsborough's other attraction is the Steeves House. William Henry Steeves, the owner of a shipbuilding company and grocery store, was one of the 37 Fathers of Confederation. He was born in this house in 1814. His parents, Heinrich and Rachel Stief were immigrants from Germany, who changed their name. The original house was built in 1812 and had only two rooms. When it was sold by W.H. Steeves, it passed through the hands of several managers of the nearby gypsum mill, who enlarged the house.

Your guided tour begins in the living room, distinctively furnished with both a desk fashioned from a pump organ and an unaltered Estey Pump Organ from the Hillsborough Baptist Church with the likeness of the organ builder and probably that of his wife carved into wood. The dining room has a fireplace surrounded by tiles imported from Germany. In the hallway is a so-called picture pocket, a picture fastened to the wall with hinges at the bottom, so that it can flip open at the top, to provide a niche for mail, bills, etc. The staircase has an unusual feature: A number of steps have prisms in them. Whenever the lady of the house required maid service,

ST. MARY'S
ANGLICAN CHURCH

she would place a lantern beneath the stairs. The light shone through the prism, signalling the maid, who lived upstairs.

The upstairs exhibits include a rope bed in the children's room. The rope had to be made taut each night, otherwise the bed would sag — thus giving rise to the saying "Good night, sleep tight." The "grapevine quilt" in the bedroom, made by Maria Steeves in 1834, received a first prize in New York. Unfortunately, a jar of jam was wrapped into it, which broke on the way back to New Brunswick. The jam stains remain. Mrs. Steeves' changing room has a pretty stencilled floor.

Your guide can also take you to nearby St. Mary's Anglican Church, built in 1886. Its architecture includes stained-glass windows and a cross, made from another, larger cross that was saved from the 1666 great fire in London, England.

MONCTON

A BRIEF HISTORY

Considering its economic history, Moncton's motto *Resurgo* (I Rise Again) was well chosen. Its original Acadian settlers were uprooted by British troops led by Lt-Col. Robert Monckton during the Seven Years' War (1756–1763) and were soon replaced by Pennsylvanian-Dutch settlers. By 1855, Scottish entrepreneurs and Irish labourers had established Moncton's first economic base — shipbuilding; when this collapsed in the next decade, Moncton became a rail centre with the completion of the Intercolonial Railway in 1872. Moncton businessmen took advantage of the federal government's protective tariff policies and subsidized freight rates to establish industries that produced goods mostly for central Canada. Neighbouring Acadian communities as well as Irish immigrants provided pools of cheap labour.

Incorporated as a city in 1890, Moncton's rail facilities over the next two decades grew to be the third largest in Canada. Hundreds of employees were lost after 1922 when Montreal became the headquarters for the recently created Canadian National Railways, but Moncton remained the rail "hub" of the Maritimes, and the CNR was its largest employer for the next two generations. In 1920, the city's economy got a major boost when the T. Eaton Company of Toronto opened a large department store and a mail order facility to serve the entire Maritimes. During the Second World War Moncton became a major airforce training and supply centre.

In Moncton, the post-war boom of the 1950s and 1960s was accompanied by another significant social change. The long and sometimes uneasy association between the anglophones and French-speaking Acadians matured into a bicultural and bilingual city. Symbolic recognition of this cultural balance came with the establishment, in 1963, of the bilingual University of Moncton. At the same time, one of the university's major advocates, the Assumption Mutual Life Insurance Company, financed the construction and development of a civic centre that included the city hall, a hotel, and a high-rise office complex. In 1968–69, the new city hall was the scene of several confrontations between the predominantly English-speaking council and university students demanding that proceedings reflect Moncton's reality as a bilingual community. Time would be on the students' side.

Within the first six months of 1976, Moncton's traditional economy collapsed. The T. Eaton Company announced the closure of its mail order centre with the loss of 3,900 jobs; the Canadian National Railways began the first of several layoffs heralding the shutting down of its sprawling shops and marshalling yards; and Ottawa indicated its intention to reduce the Canadian Forces supply depot.

MUSÉE ACADIEN

Yet, Moncton soon proved that its motto was more than a Latin phrase. It already had the Maritimes' largest shopping mall and by the late 1980s, several major communications firms had chosen Moncton to set up shop, taking advantage of the city's strategic geographical location in the Maritimes and its bilingual citizens. Moncton had "risen again."

CENTENNIAL PARK

TIDAL BORE

A WALKING TOUR

The city walk starts at the Bore Park on Main Street which offers a view of the tidal bore, a unique feature of the Petitcodiac River. Twice a day, when the tide comes in, it pushes the water back up the river. The first push comes in the form of a wave similar to those that occurr in a flash flood. Depending on the positions of the moon and sun, the wave may be either a few inches high or a floodwave. The most spectacular phenomenon requires waiting for: the transformation of a mudflat into a river under 7.3 m (24 ft.) of water. The arrival times of the tidal bore are available at the Moncton visitor centre, and on a signboard in the park.

From the park, turn left onto Main Street to walk

THOMAS WILLIAMS HOUSE, MONCTON

through the old downtown. Some old buildings, most notably the Transcript Building — the home, from 1900, of

the former newspaper company of that name — are dwarfed by modern highrises. At Keddy's Brunswick Hotel, turn right onto Highfield Street, which leads through a suburban neighbourhood to the corner of Park Street.

Here is the Thomas Williams House and tearoom, a yellow and white Victorian mansion built in 1883 by Thomas Williams, treasurer of the Intercolonial Railroad, which later became Canadian National Railways. The entrance leads to a large double parlour. All the rooms are decorated with period furniture and wallpaper. There is a triple chair in the parlour and a large dining-room table once owned by the designer of the ill-fated *Titanic*. One of the prettiest parts of the house is the upstairs hallway with its hardwood floors and an alcove.

On your way out, if you look to the rooftop you'll see the ragged remains of once-elegant wrought iron cresting on the roof. The story goes that while the Williamses were away their son developed a craving for candy. Finding none in the house, he had a brainstorm: he climbed onto the roof, took down that part of the cresting he could reach,

even try your hand at spinning and weaving. While the emphasis is on spinning wheels and looms, the collection also contains confederate money, stereoscope pictures, and a lathe. Among the many unusual items is a "temperance card," filled out and signed by an individual pledging to abstain from the consumption of alcohol.

SACKVILLE

A pretty university town with a well-known country inn, The Marshlands, Sackville offers something very special during the annual Atlantic Waterfowl Celebration. The event was first organized in 1990 by scores of volunteers. Their aim was to encourage wildlife preservation through education and nature-related activities. Activities include naturalist-led walks

SACKVILLE
WATERFOWL PARK

through the town's own Waterfowl Park, a decoy auction and duck-calling championships, hunting-related activities (a black powder shoot, a clay target shoot, retriever demonstrations), wildlife art, conservation exhibits, and a theatre performance at night.

A good way to get into the spirit is to visit some of the nature and art exhibitions located around town. Of particular interest are the duck carvings. They are judged in three categories: novice, intermediate, and open, the latter for experienced carvers. Some of the birds are unbelievably lifelike. In addition to ducks, there are replicas of owls, hawks, and various shorebirds. Those who want to actively participate in the celebration can take part in an orienteering workshop or join a tour to Johnson's Mills near Dorchester to view the flocks of migrating shorebirds.

The Black Powder Shoot takes place on the outskirts of Sackville. It's organized by local black powder clubs and is followed by a clay target shoot, open to anyone seeking to hone their skills in bird hunting.

The retriever demonstrations are held at a nearby pond. Training "birds" resembling padded rolling pins are put in the water of the pond, and the dogs are then directed by the sound of a whistle to retrieve them.

In the evening, the organizers of the celebration offer a walk through the 20 ha (50 a.) Waterfowl Park guided by a volunteer conservationist. The park was created in 1988 after a long effort and with a lot of cooperation. The CN Railway gave the right-of-way; Mount Allison University and the

MOUNT ALLISON
UNIVERSITY CAMPUS

town of Sackville provided some of the land; and Ducks
Unlimited installed the dykes and water control structure. The
whole area was once a saltmarsh, but the first dykes were
built in the 1600s when Acadians farmed here. The park is
part of the larger Tantramar Marshes, a name that stems from
the French word *tintamarre,* for the "noise" or "racket" made
by birds, taking off.

One of the plants you may see on your walk is purple
loosestrife, a prolific plant that invades wetlands, quickly
multiplies, and chokes the remaining vegetation. Recently, the
New Brunswick government issued a brochure that includes a
form for reporting locations of the plant, so that rangers can
destroy them. Here in the park, loosestrife is closely
monitored and does not seem to pose a problem yet. Much of
the vegetation is cattail and sedge. From the observation tower
you're likely to see mallards, as well as blue-winged teals and
Canada geese. You will learn about the difference between
dabblers and mallards, who reach down at the bottom to feed,
and divers, such as grebes, who dive under water and feed on
minnows and other small fish. According to naturalist Dr. Paul
Bragdon, a total of 128 species have been observed in the
park, and about two dozen actually breed here. The park also
has a muskrat house.

At the end of the day, you may want to go to the theatre,
either in a tent opposite the park entrance or at Mount
Allison's Windsor Theatre. The Live Bait Theatre Company is
full of surprises and a visit is definitely worthwhile. The
theatre company is independent of the waterfowl festival and
plays are shown thoughout the summer, from mid-June to the
end of August, from Wednesday to Saturday.

Another Sackville attraction is the Harness Shop, the
only one of its kind still operating in North America. It is a
genuine working shop. The front part of the house was
built in 1845, but a fire in 1991 caused extensive damage
on the upper floor. The shop opened in 1919 and it has
been going strong ever since. Currently, it has three
employees — they are highly trained craftsmen who make

HARNESS SHOP,
SACKVILLE

horse harnesses and collars, traditional
leather school bags, handbags, and
belts, as well as doing repairs. They
work with traditional equipment. The
sewing machine, for example, is about
70 years old. This is also the only
place in North America that still makes
straw-filled collars!

The Fundy Coastal Drive ends at
nearby Aulac. For a description of that
community, see pages 151-2.

THE ACADIAN COASTAL DRIVE

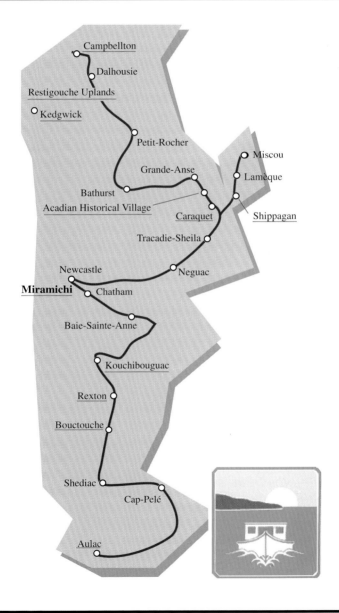

Campbellton
Dalhousie
Restigouche Uplands
Kedgwick
Petit-Rocher
Grande-Anse
Miscou
Lamèque
Bathurst
Acadian Historical Village
Caraquet
Shippagan
Tracadie-Sheila
Newcastle
Neguac
Miramichi
Chatham
Baie-Sainte-Anne
Kouchibouguac
Rexton
Bouctouche
Shediac
Cap-Pelé
Aulac

INTRODUCTION

From the forests to the sea: for today's traveller, there are few more dramatic shifts than moving from the sylvan beauty of the Matapedia Valley to the tidal estuary of the mighty Restigouche — nature's entrance to the saltwater world of New Brunswick's Acadians. Although vitally connected for three centuries to this windswept coast, the Acadians have, for generations, also been woodsmen. The sawmills of Campbellton and Dalhousie's pulp mill underscore this region's long dependency on both land and sea-based resources — a way of life that began with the Micmacs several thousand years ago.

SUGARLOAF, CAMPBELLTON

Long, graceful canoes, one of many aboriginal gifts to the white societies, often rest beside summer cottages along the Restigouche, and despite a sharply curtailed fishery, Micmac from the Cross Point Reserve just across the river from Campbellton still get their slim quota of Atlantic salmon each spring. They are also river guides par excellence for those wishing to experience a late spring run down the Restigouche.

Campbellton's Sugarloaf Mountain is a must-see spot — good hiking in summer and a skier's paradise in winter. The town's museum, besides displaying local memorabilia, contains some artifacts from the last naval engagement of the Seven Years' War — between a French frigate and a superior British force. The captain scuttled his ship in the shallow waters of the Restigouche Estuary after being trapped there.

Perhaps the most common sight along the Acadian Coastal Route is the family cottage, usually part of a cluster at the end of a road leading to the shore. In fact, they are often so close together that one must assume the occupants are good friends and neighbours.

One sign of recent prosperity is the local marina. Not all communities have them, but the one near Bathurst's Youghall Beach and another at Lower Caraquet are the locals' pride and amongst their favourite meeting places — for the weekend dance, a family birthday or just sitting around when the weather rules out a sail or cruise. The cliché about visitors being always welcome is really true in these establishments.

Signs of the area's more recent history can be seen on the drive southward towards Bathurst. Handsome farmhouses — often surrounded by modern bungalows — are reminders of the days when mixed farming was the mainstay of the economy. The new electrical generating plant at Belledune, and the ore-handling facility at a nearby dock are evidence of how times and the economy have changed.

Bathurst is perhaps the best example of this transformation. Once dominated by one of New Brunswick's earliest paper mills, its economy now includes the regional offices for several federal government departments as well as New Brunswick's largest mining operation — a base-metal complex about a half hour's drive from downtown. Besides being the main shopping area for surrounding communities, Bathurst has an outstanding golf course (Gowan Brae) close to public beaches and campgrounds set amidst a summer cottage community facing Nepisiquit Bay. The Daly Point Nature

ACADIAN VILLAGE

Reserve in Bathurst gives visitors an opportunity to view plants and animals on a salt marsh. Special attractions include the Canada geese that arrive in the fall, and the rare Maritime Ringlet butterfly.

Visitors intent on mileage rather than holidaying can take the direct highway to Chatham, but those wishing to sample perhaps the most Acadian part of New Brunswick should stick with the sea and head for Caraquet and the Acadian peninsula. From East Bathurst down as far as Pokeshaw, the residents are mostly English-speaking — the descendants of farmers and fishermen and fish processors of the late 19th-century. From Grand Anse on, you enter a French world. One sign is the style and colour of the houses: the predominant white of English communities changes to all hues of the rainbow, and the local architecture is just as varied.

Most Acadians are bilingual, and they usually welcome the chance to show off their linguistic versatility while talking about their community. And each town does, indeed, have

distinct attractions. Anse Bleue (keep going along the coast instead of turning right on the main highway) has one of the region's finest and least frequented beaches. The only other one in the same class is on Miscou Island; it has the added feature of a lighthouse that provides a superb view of Quebec's Gaspé coast.

ACADIAN VILLAGE

Caraquet is really three communities. Haut or Upper Caraquet was originally the farming section, and some still follow the land rather than the sea. Central Caraquet has always been the commercial heart and is even more so today with its handsome headquarters for the Federation of Acadian Cooperatives (Caisse Populaires), a fisheries training school, and the area's largest and busiest wharf. The annual blessing of the fishing fleet marks the start of summer for most locals. Lower or Bas Caraquet was once dependent solely on fishing. Today, the old dividing lines between the communities have almost disappeared.

Despite the recent collapse of groundfish stocks — especially cod — fishing remains a powerful economic factor, thanks in part to abundant lobster stocks and especially to snow crabs. The latter fishery began in the early 1970s, and, according to local legend, has created at least 18 millionaires. True or false, the claim helps fuel the traditional inter-town rivalry.

This is played out during the winter at the local hockey rinks but it's also evident in the constant scramble for political attention in support of local projects. In this game, Caraquet and Shippagan seemed to have fared better than the peninsula's other major centre, Tracadie. Neither of the others can match Shippagan's aquarium and marine centre, but Tracadie's leper museum is a unique testimony to a religious order's selfless dedication. Lameque's integrated fishing cooperative has few rivals, while its annual baroque music festival, now in its third decade, draws international performers and sell-out crowds. And no matter where you stop, you'll discover that the Acadian peninsula has New Brunswick's best seafood restaurants.

Anyone who first saw the area south of Tracadie, say, 20 years ago will be struck today by one thing. Communities once filled with tar-paper shacks are no more; these Acadians have indeed caught up, judging by today's neat and modern homes facing the highway all the way down from Rivière-du-Portage to Neguac. Most must commute to jobs in larger centres like Tracadie or Newcastle or spend long hours in the woods cutting pulp or at seasonal jobs at fish processing plants. Once back home, they never stop working until their biggest "soul" project is completed. Most families

POINT ESCUMINAC

will tell you how they spent every spare moment and every weekend building their homes with the help of relatives and friends. That's the Acadian way.

Once over the magnificent high-level bridge spanning the Miramichi, take the left turn marked Bay du Vin and Escuminac. Camping sites and beaches abound and thanks to most travellers' mania for "making time," the choices are many and the crowds few. Here is another area whose economy is balanced between the forest and the sea. At Bay du Vin and Escuminac, however, fishing is still the mainstay, despite its economic and physical hazards. At Escuminac, travellers often stop to pause and ponder Claude Rousell's commemorative sculpture in memory of 35 men, including fathers, sons, and cousins, who died when a freak summer storm lashed the region in 1959.

Not far past Escuminac towards Kouchibouguac National Park pass by peat moss operations, where peat moss is vacuumed, collected and packaged to be shipped as far as Japan. The beautiful Kouchibouguac National Park was created in the late 1960s from the fragile sand dunes and low-lying islands stretching northward from the estuary of the Richibucto River. It displaced Acadians, (plus a few Irish families who had intermarried with them) who had established a precarious but satisfying lifestyle fishing herring, salmon, cod, and lobster. Most of them grudgingly accepted the cash settlements offered by federal officials, but

PEAT MOSS NEAR
KOUCHIBOOUGUAC
NATIONAL PARK

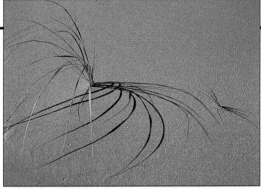

about a dozen families refused to leave. Their stand won the promise that henceforth, people aleady living within designated park boundaries will be permitted to remain there. Visitors will soon see why the residents wanted to stay.

Another worthwhile side trip is a meander around the charming little harbour town of Richibucto; then stop at the English village of Rexton (home of the Bonar Law Heritage Park), then turn right and head up the river past New Brunswick's largest Micmac reserve at Big Cove. Cross the river, return to Rexton and continue towards the coast, through Richibucto Village until the end of the road at Cape Lumière. Then get out of the car and listen to the pounding surf; buy some fresh lobsters from the processing plant and enjoy them at a picnic lunch on the sandy beach. That's the way to savour this still unspoiled world.

You can have equally relaxing soujourns simply by taking any shore road leading to Côte Ste. Anne, St. Edouard-de-Kent or Bouctouche Bay. Or alternatively the roads on either side of the Bouctouche and Cocagne rivers provide close glimpses of how Acadians have resettled rich farm lands. Many have created handsome urban retreats in a rural setting, but there are also some excellent farms that provide for the greater Moncton region.

BONAR LAW HISTORIC SITE, REXTON

Once you reach Cocagne and Shediac, you are already entering Moncton's sphere, and the signs of urban life are everywhere. The roar of high-powered hydroplanes flying across the calm surfaces of Cocagne River several weekends during the summer to the great delight of throngs of spectators is mainly a spectacle for the city dweller. So too is the sprawling cottage world that has engulfed the coastline from Cocagne, through Shediac and Pointe du Chene and on to Cap-Pelé. All summer long, cottagers and their numerous visitors play on the beaches; the warm waters of Shediac Bay teem with sailboats and powerboats; and for at least one weekend every summer, as many as 50,000 rock fans take over Parlee Beach for an ear-numbing experience.

The remaining section of the Acadian Coastal Route — through Port Elgin and Aulac — is a quieter experience, probably because its inhabitants are mostly rural English farmers. They are the direct descendants of Yorkshire settlers encouraged to come out after the land was ceded to the British in 1763 at the close of the Seven Years' War. Since that imperial conflict brought about the expulsion of over 5,000 Acadians, their descendants are less than enthusiastic about commemorating the event. That is why you are unlikely to find many Acadians wandering about the restored battlements of Fort Beausejour near Sackville. Perched on a hill, it overlooks vast marshlands created by dykes built by the very first Acadians so long ago.

ROGERSVILLE

SHEDIAC

Today's Acadians prefer to celebrate the present and the fact that they have been able to live and to prosper along one of the best stretches of coastal real estate to be found anywhere.

LA PAYS DE LA SANGOUINE, BOUCTOUCHE

MOUNT SAGAMOOK

FIRE TOWER ON TOP OF MOUNT CARLETON

MOUNT CARLETON PROVINCIAL PARK

Properly speaking, the Acadian Coastal Drive starts at Campbellton (just across the bridge from Quebec's Gaspé) and runs along the coast towards Bathurst and Caraquet. But there are some less-visited spots in the province's interior you should consider visiting, starting with Mount Carleton Provincial Park and including the villages of Kedgwick and Nictau.

Mount Carleton Provincial Park was created in 1969 as a step to preserve wilderness in New Brunswick. In the Restigouche Uplands, it is the largest provincial park in New Brunswick. Mount Carleton, at 820 m (2,693 ft.) is the highest elevation in the Maritimes. Since altitude affects climate, expect lower temperatures near the summits at any time of the year and snow from mid-October to about mid-May. Moose, black bears, and deer all live here, even though hunting pressure outside the park has been severe for many years.

The rivers and lakes in the Uplands were used as canoe routes by early inhabitants. The logging industry also used them to float timber to nearby sawmills. In the early 1900s, the area began attracting hunters and fishermen from many states and provinces. Salmon and big game were abundant. Many camps were built along the shores of the Nictau and Nepisiguit lakes to serve sportsmen.

MILLER'S CANOE FACTORY

Today, the park is open year-round for outdoor enthusiasts to enjoy fishing, birdwatching, canoeing, unsupervised swimming, and particularly hiking.

NICTAU

Off all the regular tourist routes and reached from the town of Plaster Rock by N.B. 385, in the village of Nictau, you will come across one of New Brunswick's most special small industries — the workshop of Miller's Canoes.

"I made it myself." Expect to hear that more than once from William V. Miller III while touring his unique workshop and yard. Just about everything on the premises is made from scratch. Trees are selected and cut on his own land, then sawed and left to dry for about two years. Cedar, well known for its durability, is used for the canoe's ribs and planking. White spruce makes lightweight gunnels, and various other hardwoods are also utilized. It is amazing how many moulds are crammed into his workshop, some of them dating back to 1925, when Mr. Miller's grandfather started the business.

Canoes are built around these moulds, and the production process hasn't really changed much. Wooden ribs, 3/8 of an inch thick, are put into a "steamer" (an old stove modified by the owner), in which the wood is steamed until it becomes flexible enough to be bent into any desired shape. Hanging on the wall is a wooden rib that's been bent into a knot. The ribs are then fastened to the hull with shiny brass tacks.

The next step in the process is to cover the wooden canoe with epoxy, canvas, or fiberglass. Finally, it's varnished out in the yard. Notice the picturesquely painted walls around the door at the lower part of the shop. They are the result of surplus paint and have become quite a conversation piece.

Mr. Miller builds first-class wooden canoes and kayaks. He may even offer you one to try out, especially if you own one of these department-store "Tupperware canoes," as he calls them.

135

KEDGWICK

Kedgwick is about halfway between Campbellton (on the Acadian Coastal Rout) and St. Léonard (on the St. John River Scenic Drive). Near the town is a forestry museum and park.

The huge wooden lumberman with axe and saw at the camp entrance signifies logging's traditional importance in this area. In the interpretation centre, you'll learn a little

about different uses of wood — from hardwood floors and cabinets to maple syrup, shingles, and chips. There is also information about fire prevention, and about traditional harvesting tools, such as pick poles for river drives and cant hooks, used at the mill to turn wood. A short video shows original footage of logging operations some sixty years ago — presented by the people who took part in them! For more details, we suggest Roderick Myles's *Memories: Tales from the Restigouche River*.

A small cabin next to the centre is a facsimile of the office where weekly checks were issued to the workers — $4.29 for loggers and $8.55 for teamsters. Nearby is the combined bunkhouse kitchen. The bunkhouse, with an old barrel stove, was the dormitory for up to seventy woodcutters. In the kitchen, at the other end of the building, there's a multitude of cooking implements. Three table settings illustrate the changing times: from aluminum plates used around the turn of the century, to white enamel ware in the 1930s, to plastic plates after the Second World War. Beyond are a haycamp, a stable, and a blacksmith shop, where three types of horseshoes were made, each to suit a particular activity.

Not far from the five-seater outhouse is the teamsters' camp. Why a separate camp? First of all, teamsters usually got up at 4 a.m., a bit early for lumbermen; and, since they worked with horses all day long, they needed their own facilities in which they could repair their harnesses — which is the way they usually spent their evenings. Last, but possibly not least, teamsters tended to smell of horse, something not appreciated by loggers. Beyond the camp is a fire station with fire-fighting equipment, a map of the fire towers in the region, and a warehouse.

CAMPBELLTON

As you approach the city of Campbellton from Bathurst on N.B. 11, Sugarloaf Mountain rises above its surroundings. As you drive by, its shape changes. Viewed from Campbellton, it is not a one-, but a two-peaked mountain, just like its famous namesake in Rio de Janeiro — admittedly, a pocket-sized version.

Like any mountain, the best view is from its top; if you feel the compulsion "just because it's there," drive into Sugarloaf Provincial Park.

If you hike up to the rocky summit, you're rewarded with a grand view. Far below lies Campbellton, the bridge across the Bay of Chaleur, and, beyond, rugged Gaspé, covered in distant haze. Almost everywhere else is forest. The park offers several good trails, used by hikers in the summer and by skiers and snowmobilers in the winter. Almost due south, 40 miles as the crow flies, you may be able to see the peaks of Mount Carleton Provincial Park — the top of the Restigouche Uplands including the highest peak in the Maritimes. The view from the Sugarloaf is one of the finest in Northern New Brunswick.

PRITCHARD LAKE, SUGARLOAF

VIEW FROM SUGARLOAF

THE ACADIAN HISTORICAL VILLAGE

Just a few miles outside Caraquet is one of the finest and most appealing of New Brunswick's heritage sites — the Acadian Historical Village. Just beyond the parking lot is the large Reception Centre whose modern design contrasts dramatically with the historical re-creation you are about to see on site.

The first building on the walking tour is the Mazerolle Farm. Built in 1842, the farmhouse was transported here from Mazerolle Settlement near Fredericton. At the outdoor oven a costumed guide bakes bread. The small adjoining building that looks like an outhouse actually houses the pump for the water supply. The next building on the tour is the Martin House, the oldest building in the village. It was built in 1783 as a trapper's cabin, and seven people lived in this humble dirt-floored dwelling.

Past a number of other houses, you come to the Doucet Farm, where you'll probably see a guide in period costume dying wool. She uses all natural dyes to produce colours ranging from red to blue, besides a variety of earthen tones.

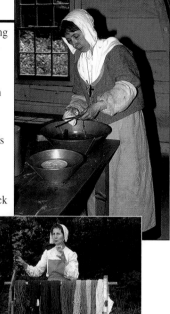

Most of the colours are obtained by boiling flowers or roots — like goldenrod, which produces a rich yellow. By the rule of thumb, one pound of flowers is used for each pound of dry wool. The blue was traditionally made by dissolving indigo in the urine of a 12- or 13-year-old boy!

The general store has beautiful glass panels imported from Belgium. There is also a tavern, and next to it the carpenter's shop. You can see the carpenter working amidst a multitude of planes and other tools of his trade. Making brooms is his specialty. He starts with the trunk of a young yellow birch, carefully shaving back thin strips of wood without cutting them off. He then folds all the strands back, ties them together and — *voilà,* a new broom! On the other side of the walkway another carpenter shows how shingles used to be made. Further on are the print shop and a small restaurant called *La table des ancêtres,* or the "Ancestor's Table." It is a great place to relax in a rustic atmosphere — the food is delicious.

HAND-DYED WOOL

Back on the main path is the blacksmith shop, circa 1866. The smith is usually busy making small implements or square-headed nails for horseshoes. He shapes the red-hot metal, dips it deep into a pail of water, and then offers the cooled product to visitors. His handmade nails are special souvenirs. Just outside the dark shop is a bridge across a small creek that's home to some white geese.

BLACKSMITH

BROOMMAKER

Beyond is the mill, also of pre-1900 vintage, which operates several times a day. From the back of the mill is a fine view of the one-room schoolhouse, the chapel, and the mid-19th-century Babineau farm. Past these buildings are the cobbler shop and the post house, from which a horse-drawn cart offers a welcome ride back to the visitors' centre.

PRINTER'S APPRENTICE

Visiting the Acadian Village will take the better part of a day. This is not just a walking tour to view a number of houses from around the province, but an opportunity to see many old crafts being practised throughout the village. More information about the Acadians can be found in Henri-Dominique Paratte's book *Acadians*, in the *Peoples of the Maritimes* Series.

CARAQUET

The Acadian Festival takes place each year on August 15 — the Catholic Feast of Assumption — which was declared the official Acadian holiday in 1884. It marks the end of a week-long celebration along the Acadian Coast. Throughout the week, church masses are held, the fishing fleet is blessed, and there are dances and plays. The culminating festival is held in Caraquet. Folk dances and a re-enactment of the Acadian Convention of 1884, at which the three main Acadian symbols were chosen — flag, anthem, and official holiday — take place in the Acadian Village during the day. Visitors should be forewarned that the village is extremely crowded on festival day, and the staff have little time to answer questions — especially in English.

The most colourful and unusual event of the festival starts at 6 p.m. on the Boulevard St. Pierre — Caraquet's main street — between the old convent and a few blocks east. This stretch is closed to vehicles and at six sharp, the organized madness begins: Tintamarre, or racket, ruckus, fracas, or whatever you care to call it. In simple words, the residents dress up and make as much noise as possible. The best part of it is that this is a real family affair, from tiny toddlers with rattles to teens with multicoloured hair, wrapped in Acadian flags, rattling pots and pans, to grandparents blowing whistles while wearing a fashionable set of cowbells. Tintamarre it is. What is a pain to the ears is a feast for the eyes. Colourful costumes enliven the scene, but the red, white, and blue of the Acadian flag dominates, whether it is worn as a dress or painted on a face. Participants in the parade, once they reach the end of the parade ground, just turn around and march back, so even if you stay in one place you can get to see it all.

TINTAMARRE,
CARAQUET

ACADIAN MUSEUM

By about seven, the riotous "parade" gives way to the folk dances held in front of the remains of the old convent. (It recently burned down.) The ruins contrast starkly with the joyful surroundings and form a dramatic backdrop for the dancers in their white and blue costumes. All folk dances are introduced by the master of ceremonies, *en français*.

THE ACADIAN MUSEUM

Part of an afternoon can be enjoyably spent at Caraquet's Acadian Museum. Along with its share of the usual implements it features some unique items. One such is an article about a foot long that resembles a brush. It turns out to be an aspergillum, or holy sprinkler, used to sprinkle holy water in the Catholic Church. This one dates back to 1818.

Next to it is an Edison movie projector from 1897, a time when movies cost 25 cents. A film starring Charlie Chaplin is still threaded in the hand-cranked machine. Most of the museum is subdivided into small booths organized according to themes, such as an agricultural exhibit with hay-making equipment and an incubator; a blacksmith shop with horseshoes and an anvil; doctor's equipment, including metal splints for broken bones; two dental chairs, one used during the Great War; a loomcrofters' corner, with loom and spinning wheel, and an entertainment centre with an old slide projector (late 19th-century) and cameras. Other exhibits include old telephones, a switchboard, and a 1910 slot machine (drop a nickel, a royal flush pays 100 cigars). And all the while, you are likely to be entertained by Acadian folk music.

SHIPPAGAN

Shippagan's leading attraction is the Shippagan's Marine Centre and Aquarium. This complex is devoted to the marine world and to the fishing industry past and present. The museum that you enter is only part of the story: upstairs there's a sophisticated marine research centre. The first exhibit likely to catch your eye is the wheelhouse of a modern fishing vessel. A far cry from the much romanticized olden days with spartan equipment, this is hi-tech for the high seas. The control panel is a bewildering

SEA ANEMONES

variety of electronic instruments and communications connections, besides the conventional wheel. It is a graphic illustration of how the fisheries business has evolved.

A number of displays on the walls explain the different types of fishing and their impact on the environment: Gill-net fishing for cod and herring; door trawling for ground fish (which is done by drawing trawl boards that stir up mud); and purse seine, used to catch herring and other fish that travel in schools. The exhibits indicate the great variety of species that populate New Brunswick waters, including crabs, shrimps, and urchins, as well as char, dogfish, halibut, and red hake.

The aquarium is home to a large variety of sea life, from the sturgeon with its spiny back to colourful sea anemones.

CONTEMPORARY FISHING BOAT, WHEELHOUSE MODEL

In the adjacent auditorium a 20-minute show outlines the development of the fishing industry on New Brunswick's shores. It describes how, after the French were defeated in 1760, French-speaking Jersey entrepreneurs gained control over the industry for almost a century, employing Acadian fishermen. They practised the barter system, whereby the

Acadians delivered their catch to the company in exchange for goods from the company store. In the 19th century,

Americans began fishing in the bay, in competition with the Jersey company, which folded in this century.

There's also an outdoor aquarium, where seals often stretch lazily in the sun. They'll become active around feeding time at 11:00 a.m. and 4:00 p.m. They stay outside even in the wintertime, when they are joined by three of their fellows from the Huntsman Aquarium in St. Andrews.

KOUCHIBOUGUAC NATIONAL PARK

Kouchibouguac National Park is quite unlike New Brunswick's other National Park — Fundy. It is slightly bigger than Fundy, (240 km2 [92 sq. mi.]) but the major difference is the topography and ecosystem. Whereas Fundy has a rugged coast with windswept coastal softwoods and hardwood ridges, Kouchibouguac is basically flat land shaped by glaciation. It has bogs, salt marshes, and its major drawing card — sand dunes, seashore, and beaches. To some, the waters of the Northumberland Strait are not exactly warm, but the

TOP: SALT MARSH, KOUCHIBOUGUAC
ABOVE: BUNCHBERRIES

shallow lagoons may reach 20° C (68° F) in the summer. Major activities — other than swimming, beachcombing, and simply enjoying the beaches — are biking, canoeing, birding, and some hiking.

Kouchibouguac has two campgrounds (reserve in advance, because the campsites fill quickly) as well as a few primitive campsites that can be reached only on foot, by bike, or by canoe. There is also a restaurant and a canteen in the park. Established in 1969, the park derives its name from a Micmac word, meaning "river of the long tides."

SCULPTURE AT KOUCHIBOUGUAC NATIONAL PARK

REXTON

Rexton's Bonar Law Historic Site is a small farm that consists of the house, barns with animals, farming implements, and a garden. It is picturesquely located on the

bank of the Richibucto River. In 1850, the Rev. James Law purchased the nine hectare (22 acre) farm and established a Presbyterian manse. It was the boyhood home of Bonar Law, one of the reverend's seven children, who became the Prime Minister of Britain. Another son, Robert, lived here until 1911. He was the last of the Law family to leave the area, which fell into economic decline in the 1880s as wooden sailing ships were replaced by iron steamers.

The furniture in the house all dates back to 1875–80. Near the entrance is a "beggar's bench"; it opens into a bed — a useful feature for unexpected guests. Photographs show women applying the finishing touches to a fine quilt or doing other handiwork. One of the barns houses an 1899 thrasher, ice breakers for ice fishing, a turnip cutter, and a number of other period implements. There are also farm animals such as sheep, pigs, and turkeys.

Back at the house, your guide may offer you some homemade biscuits and tea. If you bring a lunch, there's a scenic picnic site beside the Richibucto River.

MUSEUM AND CONVENT, BOUCTOUCHE

BOUCTOUCHE

A short distance beyond the small town of Bouctouche is a relic from a time when status was not so much measured by money, but depended on standing in the community and upbringing. The walls of the Kent County Museum and Old Convent recall those times not so long past. The stately building sits amidst green lawns, next to where the old church used to be. It, in turn, was beside the graveyard. Birth, baptism, marriage, parenthood, and death were all events directly involving the church. The church also took

a keen interest in both the temporal and spiritual education of its youth — hence the convent.

Your guided tour starts in the parlour where the girls would meet their parents. About 80 girls were enrolled in this school; two-thirds of them lived in the convent and the others were day students from Bouctouche. The room next to the parlour was the office of Mother Superior, probably the most feared place in the convent. There was an old telephone here. When one of the girls was called to the phone it always was an emergency, more often than not a death in the family. The other reason a student would be summoned to the office was for punishment, which usually meant "the strap."

Life in the convent was strictly regulated: rise; Mass; breakfast; classes; lunch; afternoon classes; Mass; garden work; about an hour of leisure time; to bed at 9 p.m. And it was not free either. In 1930, accommodation and tuition cost $14 per month, music $20 and bed 50 cents. The small library could be used for another 50 cents per year. Most girls who graduated from the convent became teachers. The writing on the blackboard shows that neatness was demanded. In the upper left corner of every page they wrote on, students had to write the acronym JMJ — Jesus, Mary, and Joseph. The girls' uniforms exhibited in the classroom show the evolution of convent dress: first a dull black and white gown, later a bit of lace, and in the final days a blue outfit. The convent closed its doors in 1964.

SANDBAR,
BOUCTOUCHE

From the classroom, your tour guide takes you to the chapel. Just outside its doors is a priest's gown. Traditional gowns were much more elaborate on the back than the front because until

1969, the priest faced the altar when reading Mass, so that only his back was seen by the congregation. The chapel's white altar exhibits gothic elements. The columns had a leaf pattern on them, until a priest decided that the word and the message were more important than appearance and had the entire chapel repainted — in uniform beige. Attempts to remove the layer of paint without destroying the older pattern were successful only in two small areas that give a glimpse of the original design. The original stencilled wall decoration remains throughout the chapel.

LE PAYS DE LA SANGOUINE, BOUCTOUCHE

A short distance away, at the edge of town, is the new Pays de la Sagouine theme park. It is based on Antonine Maillet's story about a scrub woman named *La Sagouine* and her lamentations and view of the world. In the visitor centre you can watch a short bilingual film presentation about *La Sagouine* and the Acadians. A nearby wooden tower provides a view of the park and the surrounding area, including a natural island and a long, winding boardwalk that leads to it. On the way to the island, are some houses that figure in the story of *La Sagouine*. At times, Acadian music is performed and a rendition given in French of a monologue from the story.

AULAC

Right next to the border of New Brunswick and Nova Scotia, at the terminus of the Acadian Coastal Route and the Fundy Coastal Drive, is the town of Aulac and a fort where world

powers once fought for dominance in North America. In the early 1750s, England and France had achieved an uneasy peace in Europe, but this meant precious little in the faraway colonies. England began building forts throughout Nova Scotia in order to protect its settlements. One was Fort Lawrence. The French responded by building Fort Beausejour nearby. It underwent several construction stages. In 1751, it was only a palisade which was strengthened in 1752 when hostilities seemed imminent.

In 1754, a secretary at Fort Beausejour informed the British about French military plans. The British decided to attack first. When the French learned about the impending attack, they sent an appeal for help to Fortress Louisbourg in Nova Scotia. At the same time, they prepared for the attack by burning all wooden structures that might ignite under cannonfire. The British attack was launched from 38 boats that sailed up Chignecto Bay, carrying 2,000 militia,

along with cannons, and supplies. In early June, the British began their siege — digging trenches and bringing cannons into position. News arrived from Fortress Louisbourg that no reinforcements would be sent, and when a direct hit destroyed one of Fort Beausejour's casemates, the French surrendered. The victorious British forces renamed the structure Fort Cumberland.

It again became prominent during the American War of Independence when a small group of revolutionaries attacked it. The fort was damaged but withstood the attack. The same summer, 200 Yorkshire settlers arrived to

restore the damaged fort and defend the British colony against the American forces.

Today, names on mailboxes such as Yeoman, Black, Truman, Dixon, and Keillor are reminders of these Yorkshire families. Fort Cumberland was briefly used again in the war of 1812; after that, it fell into disrepair until it was declared a National Historic Park in 1926. Extensive diggings have been undertaken to show today's visitors the outline and some of the details of the original fort.

Your tour starts in the visitor centre and museum where some artifacts from the fort are displayed. There are seven original paintings by Lewis Parker depicting scenes of the fort from 1754 to 1778. A short slide show depicts the circumstances of the British attack from a French perspective. There are Acadian artifacts, such as a pair of huge sabots (wooden shoes) and a rush light — a cattail dipped in animal fat, clipped upright into position and then lighted. The museum also boasts what is reputed to be the smallest book in the world, a 3/4 x 1/2-inch volume containing 100 pages of extremely thin paper. It is a

Schloss' English Bijou Almanac. Other artifacts relate to the Micmac Indians, the railroads, and dyke building.

The fort is built in the traditional star-shape. From the top of the walls, you can see in its interior the remains of stone casemates and barracks. You can also explore casemates with storerooms underneath the walls of the fort. Looking out from the fort, you have a panoramic view across the marshes.

LEWIS PARKER PAINTINGS, FORT CUMBERLAND

MIRAMICHI RIVER ROUTE

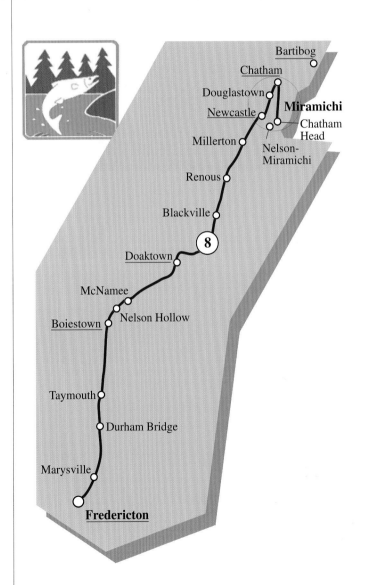

Bartibog

Chatham

Douglastown

Miramichi

Newcastle

Chatham Head

Millerton

Nelson-Miramichi

Renous

Blackville

8

Doaktown

McNamee

Nelson Hollow

Boiestown

Taymouth

Durham Bridge

Marysville

Fredericton

SALMON FISHING IN
THE MIRAMICHI

INTRODUCTION

Entering the Miramichi region of New Brunswick is almost a step back into the 19th century. The region is steeped in history of that age, when the economy and most other human activities revolved around the forest. As historian Stewart McNutt described those times, "All the commerce and industry of the province had become secondary to the timber trade.... The valley of the Miramichi now held the reputation of offering the best opportunities for those searching for the great stands of pine timber that were becoming so much more elusive."

By mid-century, the great pine stands were no more, but a new harvest in the form of sawn lumber awaited the axes and saws of the Irish and Scots who provided the muscle and the character of the Miramichi lumber industry — and still do. They worked for one of several powerful British-born or old-country-connected entrepreneurs who viewed the Miramichi as their private preserve. According to a recent study, "Douglastown, Chatham, and to a degree, other towns along the Bay of Chaleur and Gulf of St. Lawrence coasts that fell within the orbit of Pollock, Gilmour and Company or (until his bankruptcy in 1849) Joseph Cunard grew essentially as company towns, dependent upon the mills and mercantile enterprises of their leading entrepreneur.... Opportunities for small-scale, independent lumbering had vanished."

They would never return. When the pulp and paper era began in the 1880s, it was the same story: outsiders from either Upper Canada, the U.S. or Great

RANKIN HOUSE,
DOUGLASTOWN

Britain, provided the capital and the bosses for the mills built initially in and around Chatham. The labour was supplied by Irish and Scots who had migrated to the Miramichi over the previous two generations. They either lived in villages close to the larger centres like Chatham, Douglastown, and Newcastle, or further upriver where they became the woodcutters and rivermen who guided the winter's harvest down to the mills during the spring freshets.

The river drives are no more. Heavily laden pulp trucks now fill the local highways, and the skilled axemen have been replaced by chainsaw operators with their noisy but far more efficient equipment. Some still work out of remote lumber camps but the great majority commute daily to the cutting areas.

We tend to look back wistfully at those days, regretting the loss of a more robust and colourful era. Certainly, during the drives, the old Miramichi came alive with the shouts and actions of incredibly agile lumberjacks as they guided the logs downstream and broke up jams. The communities along the way came alive too when the drives ended and the men hit the taverns with their season's pay.

Fortunately, those boisterous times live on in song. And they survive in large measure because of the initiative of the Miramichi's most famous son, Max Aitken, whose father was a local clergyman. Like so many other young men, Aitken left his family home in Newcastle at an early age to seek his fortune. Unlike the vast majority, he found it as a financier and newspaper baron in London. He was made a lord, and took his title, "Beaverbrook," from a Miramichi hamlet he had known as a child.

MIRAMICHI RIVER

In the 1940s, Beaverbrook became intensely interested in his roots, and even though he remained an influential figure in London's political and financial worlds for the rest of his life, he began to make longer and longer summer visits to his beloved Miramichi. He asked the local librarian, Louise Manny, one of his childhood school friends, to try to collect some of the old lumbermen's songs he had heard as a boy. Knowing next to nothing about them, she let it be known through the local newspaper and in notices posted around town that she planned a gathering at the Legion

Hall. Anyone who knew any songs was urged to attend and have them recorded.

The response so impressed Miss Manny that she became fascinated with local folksongs. She began a 15-minute Sunday afernoon program on the local radio station, where for the next 20 years, she played from her continually growing collection of recordings of woodsmen and farmers singing what Maine's renowed folklorist Sandy Ives calls "the old come-all-ye's in the old unaccompanied way." In 1958, Louise Manny organized the Miramichi Folksong Festival, where for three nights scores of the people she had recorded performed on stage at Newcastle's (now Miramichi) townhall. The singing and these annual festivals have never stopped. And for the rest of her life, neither did Louise Manny. Besides directing the festival, she supervised the restoration of a pioneer Miramichi burying ground and converted Lord Beaverbrook's boyhood home, the old Presbyterian manse, into what is now the Old Manse Library, where she served as librarian until her retirement in 1967. In that same year, she was named one of the "Women of the Century" by the National Council of Jewish Women of Canada. Her citation read: "More than any other single person, Dr. Manny is responsible for the preservation and perpetuation of the history and folklore of eastern New Brunswick.... She preserved for future generations glimpses of the past that might otherwise have been lost."

LORD BEAVERBROOK'S BOYHOOD HOME

Newcastle's annual Folk Festival has become its major annual tourist event, which was one of the main reasons that its longtime rival, neighbouring Chatham, introduced the Irish Festival.

Their rivalry, at times friendly and at other times less so, dates back to the turn of the century when Chatham (now Miramichi) was *the* town on the Miramichi. Its success in convincing outside investors to build the area's first pulp mill in 1889 led to a second mill being constructed on the Miramichi a mile below Chatham.

MIRAMICHI FOLKSONG FESTIVAL

By contrast, Newcastle, whose economic mainstay was its sawmills, was languishing. Census statistics for 1901 showed that Newcastle's industries were capitalized at $177,585,

compared to Chatham's $1,008,340. Alarmed by this economic stagnation, Newcastle's leading merchants incorporated the town in 1899 and tried to attract new industries such as furniture factories and pulp mills by offering tax incentives and other bonuses. The sawmill owners were decidedly unenthusiastic, fearing that pulp mills in particular would threaten their monopoly of local labour and raw material.

This tug-of-war went on for years, with neighbouring towns vying for new businesses and pulp and sawmill owners competing for timber rights. Today, brought together in one municipal unit of Miramichi City, Newcastle is the pulp mill centre: one look at the vast pile of pulpwood outside the mill is the best proof. Chatham, however, has fallen behind and despite repeated efforts, has never been able to find a reliable economic mainstay.

Despite these setbacks, there's a great natural resource — found in the Miramichi River itself — that benefits all the communities on both sides of its tree-lined banks. Since the first settlers, Miramichiers have looked forward to a spring bonanza — the migrating Atlantic salmon. It was a secret that couldn't be kept, and by the 1920s, after the pulp mill industry was firmly established, the locals found a lucrative sideline — guiding sports fishermen eager to experience the thrill of reeling in a 9kg–13kg (20–30 lb.) salmon, one of the best fighting fish anywhere.

Up along the several branches of the Miramichi, the rich and often the famous made their annual pilgrimages to "the camp" — well-appointed, even luxurious fishing lodges located on or near salmon pools exclusively reserved for members' use. Over the years, small towns like Blackville and Doaktown developed facilities to serve the needs of these wealthy visitors, thus creating more jobs. A special kind of tourism had arrived on the Miramichi, a depression-proof one, so long as the mighty salmon kept returning every spring.

And they did — until about twenty years ago. Both locals and visiting "sports" had grown accustomed to good and bad fishing years, but gradually the bad ones became the norm, and salmon

IRISH FESTIVAL, MIRAMICH

conservation groups (notably the Atlantic Salmon Federation) and the provincial government, took action to save the salmon. Strict fishing quotas were imposed, and when the fish scarcity continued, a hook-and-release policy was added. As well, a major publicity campaign was launched to support political efforts to curb and eventually to all but eliminate commercial salmon fishing both in New Brunswick and in places like Greenland and Newfoundland on the salmon's migration route. At the same time, pulp-mill owners have spent millions to reduce effluents flowing into the Miramichi in a belated attempt to make up for the dirty and wasteful practices of the past.

Throughout all these changes and challenges, the mighty Miramichi River system continues to symbolize New Brunswick past and present. Travelling along the Miramichi River route is more than a voyage through time. Besides reaching into the very centre of New Brunswick, both geographically and historically, travellers become aware of the silent presence of this magnificent waterway just beyond that row of trees, or below the high-level bridge at Doaktown. If the river could talk, it would be a tale of log drives and jams, of salmon strikes and escapes, of mills along its banks, and the odd farm as well.

Fortunately, we can hear the river's story through the songs of Wilmot MacDonald and Nick Underhill recorded by Louise Manny a generation ago — lusty songs about love and life in the Miramichi woods: songs still being sung by performers at the Miramichi Folk Song Festival.

And life along the Miramichi is being preserved in another form. David Adams Richards has become one of Canada's most widely read authors by writing award-winning novels based on the people he grew up with — the people of the Miramichi. Herb Curtis's trilogy, *The Americans Are Coming*, *The Last Tasmanian*, and *Lone Angler*, describing the humorous exploits of some young salmon guides is also adding to the mystique of the Miramichi River and the region of which it is the heart.

RITCHIE'S WHARF, MIRAMICHI

BARTIBOG

In Bartibog, a few miles from Mirimichi, you'll find the appealing MacDonald Farm Historic Site. From the visitor centre walk on a winding woods trail down to open fields and the coast. The land is not much different from when

Alexander MacDonald settled here. He previously served as a private soldier with the British Forces in the War of Independence. He became a justice of the peace and, in his day, could be considered well off. The property stayed in the family until 1853, when it was sold.

The seven-room farmhouse was home for MacDonald, his wife, and their 13 children. It was constructed with

BARTIBOG HERITAGE FARM

stones that came from Scotland as ballast. Jellies and jams from the olden days, still preserved by a thick layer of wax, line some kitchen shelves. There is also a spice canister with a lock, suggesting how precious spices were in those days. The plates in the hutch are probably from Scotland, they have been dated to the 18th century. The soap in those days was homemade from beef fat, lye, and water. The adjacent

sitting room is bright and airy, with a carved checkerboard and tobacco twists that look like braids. Upstairs you'll be amazed by a seven-foot gun used for waterfowl hunting. A hunter needed a steady hand for that piece!

Back outside, enjoy the beautiful view across the Miramichi Bay. This is a choice spot for today's visitors. The original settlers had to work hard to make productive farmland out of the dense forests. The wharf and the spring house next to the bay provide wonderful photographic opportunities. And what would a farm be without animals! There are horses, goats, pigs, turkeys, and the occasional cat — a perfect backdrop for an early 19th century farm.

MIRAMICHI

IRISH FESTIVAL

The Lord Beaverbrook arena in Miramichi-Chatham, site of the festival, is fittingly decorated in orange and green, with a neutral white separating the two. Not surprisingly, green dominates. Along the walls are stalls, hawking art, tapes with Irish music, books on Irish heritage, rings, mostly green crafts, Irish tourism, and printouts of genealogical information regarding Irish names. After the short opening ceremonies, the music begins. Some bands have "gone electric," but most musicians prefer traditional instruments, like banjo, mandolin, accordion, and harp. The music ranges from toe-tappin' tunes like "Whiskey in the Jar," ballads such as "Sam Hall," "Black Velvet Band," and "Four Green Fields," to rebel songs like "The Rising of the Moon," and songs of everyday life such as "Biddy Mulligan."

The nearby Dr. Loisier Junior High School hosts other events: book launchings, special interest workshops about tin whistles, Irish dancing, traditional Irish music, and lectures on descendants of Irish immigrants. More information on the Irish at a glance is found in Peter McGuigan's book *Irish*, in *The Peoples of the Maritimes* Series.

The early immigrants, who are being celebrated and were responsible for these festivities, had little fun themselves during the early years. Irish settlers started coming to the Maritimes in large numbers in 1847 in search of a better life. 1848 and 1849 were the worst years of the potato famine in Ireland, and without sufficient aid from the mainland, they had little choice but to flee in ever greater numbers. At least one million had left Ireland by 1851 for North America. Many died on the long trip, and the Irish festival celebrates the contributions these settlers and their descendants have made.

THE MIRAMICHI FOLK SONG FESTIVAL

Each year, the week-long festival begins with the very popular fiddling contest, featuring well-known performers such as North America's only championship fiddle team, Graham and Eleanor Townsend. Then there are afternoon performances and nightly shows with popular performers such as Aubrey Hanson, founder of the New Brunswick Country Music Hall of Fame in Fredericton, bluegrass fiddler Eddie Poirier from Moncton, fiddlers Ivan and Vivian Hicks, fiddler Gordon Stobbe, and banjo man George Hector. For years now, festival organizers have put together a program that offers something for every taste. Little wonder that the festival, one of the longest running folksong festivals in North America, is so popular.

Many events take place in the Lord Beaverbrook auditorium in Miramichi-Newcastle. It usually fills up early. Most of the performers play two or three tunes, which allows for a wide variety of styles during the show. And different styles they are: from sad ballads of lost love by Sir Walter Scott to thigh-slappin' bluegrass tunes; from medleys of war songs to the thoughtful "Streets of London," and Irish drinking songs. Also very popular are old and contemporary songs about the Miramichi River. But the perennial favorites are fiddle tunes, played by local and internationally known performers. "Maple Sugar," "Turkey in the Straw," "Don Messer's Breakdown," and "Tennessee Waltz" are just a few in a seemingly endless list of well-appreciated tunes. The "Orange Blossom Special" on twin fiddles is the greatest crowd pleaser. After the show, there's an opportunity to talk to some of the performers and purchase tapes and CDs. A good collection of New Brunswick folksongs is found in *Folksongs of New Brunswick* by Edward Ives.

THE MIRAMICHI HIGHLAND GATHERING

Ah, the Highlands! Images of heath-covered mountains, peat-burning stoves in thatch-covered cottages, a lonesome kilt-clad man playing the pipes, Bonnie Prince Charlie, ... well, almost. The Highland Society of New Brunswick at Miramichi was founded in 1842, and holds its annual

Highland Gathering in late August. The festivities traditionally get under way at the Rankin House in Douglastown on Saturday with a band concert, the official opening ceremonies, and outdoor entertainment.

As the next activities are still a couple of hours away, take the opportunity to have a look at the Rankin House. Georgian in style with a Greek Revival portico, it was built in 1837 by Alexander Rankin, owner of a lumbering and shipbuilding business. In 1891, the building became an elementary school and it was used as such until 1979 when the Historical Society began restoring the house. The schoolroom display reflects the building's early days. In the corner of the ballroom is a little circus merry-go-round, built from oil stove and blender motors by Frank Aubie, a local inventor who "just loved to build things."

The museum also houses various displays relating to the shipbuilding days on the Miramichi.

Afterwards, drive to the nearby Miramichi-Newcastle Town Square where pipes and drums play. They'll continue throughout the day at various locations in Newcastle and Chatham and also at night in the Civic Centre.

The next day the festival continues at the MacDonald Farm Historic Site in Bartibog. Frenzied activities develop all around the house: peddlers unwrap their wares under the tents on the big lawn of the house; musicians strum their guitars and pluck their fiddles on the stage next to the many picnic tables; pipers and drummers rehearse their tunes; and in the back of the house, a few big athletes loosen up for the events to come. And you can take the time for a tour of the historic house, complete with cookies and tea.

Once the program gets under way, bands from all over
the province perform Scottish folk tunes. You can also find
out about your genealogy or buy wares from Scotland.
Sportsmen usually explain and demonstrate some of the
ancient sports that remain part of any highland game: the
throwing of a stone, or the Scottish hammer, once used for
destroying bridges; or the ultimate Scottish event—the
tossing of the caber.

And all the while the pipes and drums are playing,
tuneful reminders of the mist-covered highlands, the
valleys and the glens back where many New Brunswickers
came from. More about Scottish people at a glance can be
found in Emmerson's *Scots*, in the *The Peoples of the
Maritimes* Series.

DOAK HISTORIC SITE

DOAKTOWN

In the village of Doaktown, the Doak Historic Site is well worth a visit. From the entrance to the site, a guide takes you across fields to the white clapboard house of the Doaks. Construction of the house was begun in the 1820s by Robert Doak, whose career reads like this: 1822, overseer of the poor; 1823, supervisor in charge of highways; 1825, justice of the peace; 1826, school trustee; 1829, acting coroner. The Doak family came from Scotland. Due to a storm, they sought shelter in the harbour of Newcastle and soon changed their plans: rather than settle in Kentucky, they stayed in New Brunswick.

You enter the house through the kitchen, which is full of artifacts from the early 1800s: a table whose legs are stained with pig's blood; a citronella plant used against mosquitoes; deer antlers for a coat hanger; and a multi-purpose day bed that can also be used to store items that would otherwise be in the way. Things were simpler then, but certainly functional. Even the geraniums in the window have a second purpose: to deter flies. A narrow stairway leads up to the field hands' quarters. This room is quite bare, its only remarkable feature being the oversized spinning wheel. Back downstairs, the living room contains a piano organ, and an old gramophone — items that indicate the wealth of the inhabitants. The adjacent room with the solid wood window shutters was Mrs. Doak's domain. The sewing room has been similarly secured. She feared Indian attacks, and wanted the shutters for protection.

Upstairs is the boys' room and another room for a live-in minister. Mr. Doak founded what was later to become the United Church in this area. The minister's room has painted floors, another sign of wealth, and a bed painted green and pink. It is noteworthy that the furniture in the Doak house is original and not collected from various buildings as at other heritage sites in New Brunswick.

The next stop is the large barn not far from the house. This is quite a lively place during the summer

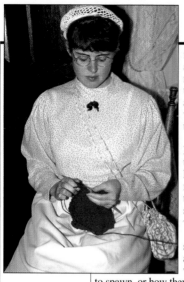

months, when the barn houses some animals that spend the winter on a nearby farm. Before completing the tour, take a last look over the fields and the cedar-fence bordered path, where horses still draw wagons, now taking visitors around the fields.

Doaktown's other attraction is the Miramichi Salmon Museum. By the time you leave this museum you'll know that the Atlantic salmon is to most other fish as a Stradivarius is to the fiddle. Your education is conducted subtly — to the sounds of splashing water and the clicking of a fishing reel.

First you learn about the life cycle of salmon: from alevin to fry, parr, smolt, and grilse. Scientists are still not certain why salmon return to their parent rivers to spawn, or how they find their way back from the distant waters of Greenland, where they go to feed on small fish and crustaceans. Unlike Pacific salmon, which spawn once and then die, Atlantic salmon often spawn two or three times. While in the river to spawn, salmon eat nothing. The nest or redd is dug by the female in gravel, where the eggs are deposited — about eight hundred eggs per pound of her body weight. They are then fertilized by the milt from the male salmon. The cycle of life has begun once more.

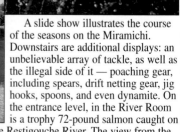

SALMON MUSEUM, DOAKTOWN

A slide show illustrates the course of the seasons on the Miramichi. Downstairs are additional displays: an unbelievable array of tackle, as well as the illegal side of it — poaching gear, including spears, drift netting gear, jig hooks, spoons, and even dynamite. On the entrance level, in the River Room is a trophy 72-pound salmon caught on a fly in 1990 in the Restigouche River. The view from the River Room across the Miramichi is fantastic. Outside are a few cabins, an aquarium with salmon and other fish species, a smoke house, boat house, ice and snow house, and a guide's camp. The tour emphasizes the importance of the Atlantic salmon as a source of food and trade in past and present. Equally important is the fact that this prized fish is a part of the natural chain, whose habitat must be protected for its survival.

BOIESTOWN

Lumbering is one of the most important industries in New Brunswick, and the Central New Brunswick Woodmens' Museum in Boiestown is devoted to the history and evolution of logging. To call it a museum is something of a misnomer. It's more of a heritage park, with several buildings housing a variety of displays. The trademark of the park are two Quonset huts in the shape of half logs with an axe and a cant hook, or "peavey."

The tour starts with a look at a huge sculpture (by Marilyn Farrell) depicting 19th century logging, and some trophies. In an adjacent room are pictures and sculptures by Indians from the Big Cove and Red Bank reserves as well as finely detailed models of horse-drawn sleds with piles of timber. Exhibits in this room change each year. The many buildings on the premises include a wheelwright's shop, machine sheds with farm tractors (including a 1917 Fordson tractor from England), as well as a bunkhouse and an adjacent cookhouse. The large beds were used by ten men at a time with the youngest member of the team getting a space at one of the edges. Not a good arrangement: the outside sleeper had only one side warmed by his fellow lumbermen whereas insiders were kept warm from both sides.

167

Also on the site is a 100-year-old trapper's cabin with a variety of traps — humane and otherwise. Another building houses an impressive collection of saws. Early crosscut saws frequently got stuck in the wood because they did not get the sawdust out of the cut. Around 1880, the raker tooth was invented to accomplish that task — thus making sawing a lot easier. A few decades later, technology made a big step forward with the invention of motorized chain saws. The museum displays an impressive collection of saws, ranging from early models to modern Oregon saws, used for very big trees.

A different kind of exhibit is the former ore train, whose locomotive is expertly operated by engineer Vernon Dunphy. Your ride takes you by the trout pond, and before you have a chance to ask if there are fish in it, Vernon throws in a handful of feed. There's a wild splashing for a second or two, and then only the ripples remain. One of the special events organized at the museum is the annual fishing derby, where novices and experts alike can try their skill. The little train steams up an incline, reaches a fire tower and the watchman's cabin, before descending again past an Indian teepee and a group of wooden black bears to the station. It's a memorable 15-minute trip. From Boisetown you can continue along N.B. 8 to Fredericton (pages 68-73) where you meet the St. John River Scenic Drive.

CONTENTS

GETTING THERE

BY LAND

The Trans Canada Highway enters New Brunswick from Quebec. Follow the Trans-Canada Highway, Interstate 95, or a host of routes from the New England States and Quebec that connect to the New Brunswick Scenic routes and highway network. Visitors from the United States must pass through Canada Customs checkpoints before entering the country.

Greyhound from New York (1-800-231-2222) and Voyageur from Montreal (613-238-5900) connect with SMT bus lines in New Brunswick (506-458-6000).

VIA Rail Canada (1-800-561-3926) provides train service via Montreal and via Halifax to New Brunswick. Places served are Sackville, Moncton, Newcastle, Bathurst.

BY SEA

There are several options for car-ferry trips.

Portland, Maine, to Yarmouth, Nova Scotia
Daily service by MS *Scotia Prince* from early May through October. Reservations required. In Canada: Box 609, Yarmouth, N.S., B5A 4B6. In the U.S.A.: *Prince of Fundy* Cruises Limited, Box 4216, Station A, Portland, Maine, 04101. In U.S.A. and Canada call toll-free 1-800-341-7540; in Maine, 1-800-482-0955.

Bar Harbor, Maine, to Yarmouth, Nova Scotia
Daily service from mid-June to mid-September aboard the MV *Bluenose*. Tri-weekly service during the off-season. In Canada: Marine Atlantic/Reservations, Box 250, North Sydney, N.S., B2A 3M3; 902-794-5700. In the U.S.A.: Terminal Supervisor, Marine Atlantic, Bar Harbor, Maine, 04609; 1-800-341-7981.

Digby, Nova Scotia to Saint John, New Brunswick
Daily service across the Bay of Fundy aboard the MV *Princess of Acadia*; three trips daily during peak season. Marine Atlantic Reservations, Box 250, North Sydney, N.S., B2A 3M3; 902-794-5700. In the U.S.A., 1-800-341-7981.

Prince Edward Island to New Brunswick
Marine Atlantic operates a year-round daily ferry service between Cape Tormentine, New Burnswick (near the N.S. border), and Borden, Prince Edward Island. No reservations.

Newfoundland to North Sydney, Nova Scotia
Twice-daily, six-hour passage from Port-Aux-Basques to North Sydney (four times daily during peak). Bi-weekly 13-hour passage from Argentia to North Sydney, mid-June through mid-September only. Marine Atlantic/Reservations, Box 250, North Sydney, N.S., B2A 3M3; 902-794-5700. In the U.S.A., 1-800-341-7981.

BY AIR

Both Air Canada (1-800-563-5151) and Canadian Airlines International (1-800-665-1177) provide daily flights to New Brunswick from most Canadian cities. Major airports in New Brunswick are located in Moncton, Saint John, Fredericton, Charlo, Chatham, Saint-Leonard and Bathurst. Affiliated regional carriers Air Nova and Air Atlantic offer scheduled connections within Atlantic Canada and flights to select destinations in the eastern United States. Car rentals may be arranged at all airports.

Limousine service is available from the terminal buildings.

TRAVEL ESSENTIALS

MONEY

American currency can be exchanged at any New Brunswick bank at the prevailing rate. Units of currency are similar to those of the United States excepting the Canadian two-dollar and one-dollar coins (the "Loonie").

Traveller's cheques and major U.S. credit cards are accepted throughout New Brunswick, although you may require cash in some rural areas. Traveller's cheques in Canadian funds can be purchased in the U.S. Cheques issued by Visa, American Express, and Thomas Cook are widely recognized.

American visitors may also use bank or credit cards to make cash withdrawals from automated teller machines that are tied into international networks such as Cirrus and Plus. These can be found in larger centres throughout the province.

PASSPORTS

Because American citizens and permanent residents routinely enter Canada, there are few restrictions. Passports and visas are not required, although some proof of citizenship or residency might be (a birth certificate or Alien Registration Card will serve). At the border, expect to be asked where you live, why you are coming to Canada, and for how long.

Citizens of other countries should check with the nearest Canadian embassy or consulate regarding entry requirements. If under 18 and unaccompanied by an adult, you must bring written permission of parent or guardian to travel in Canada. U.S. drivers' licenses are valid for operating a motor vehicle in New Brunswick.

CUSTOMS

Arriving
New Brunswick Border Customs Offices: (Area code 506)
Andover 273-2073
Centreville 276-3519
St. Croix 784-2225
Woodstock 328-9988
Campobello Island 752-2432
St. Stephen 466-2363
Clair 992-2124
Edmundston 735-5292
Grand Falls/Grand-Sault 473-3553
Saint-Leonard 423-6282
Visitors to Canada may bring certain

duty-free items into the country as part of their personal baggage. These items must be declared to Customs upon arrival and may include up to 200 cigarettes, 50 cigars, and 0.9 kilograms (2 lb.) of tobacco. Visitors are also permitted 1.14 litres (40 oz.) of liquor or wine, or 8.2 litres (24 12-ounce cans or bottles) of beer.

Gift items — excluding tobacco and alcohol products — for Canadian residents that do not exceed $40 are also duty-free. Packages should be marked "Gift" and the value indicated.

Boats, trailers, sporting equipment, cameras, and similar big-ticket items may enter Canada free of duty. However, Canada Customs may require a refundable deposit to ensure that these goods are not sold for profit. It might be better to register such items with customs officials in your own country, so that when you re-enter you have evidence that they were not bought in Canada.

Some items are strictly controlled in Canada. Firearms are prohibited, with the exception of rifles and shotguns for hunting purposes. Plant material will be examined at the border. Veterinarians certificates are required for all pets.

For further information on Canadian customs information, contact Revenue Canada, Customs and Excise, Public Relations Branch, Ottawa, Ont., K1A 0L5; 613-993-0534.

Departing
Visitors from the U.S. who have been out of the country for a minimum of 48 hours may take back goods to the value of US $400 without paying duty (provided no part of the exemption has been used within the previous 30 days). Family members may pool their exemptions. There are restrictions on alcohol and tobacco products, among others. Visitors may bring back one litre (34 oz.) of alcohol free of duty and up to 200 cigarettes and 100 non-Cuban cigars.To find out more about U.S. Customs regulations and what other restrictions and exemptions apply contact your local customs office or the U.S. Customs Service, Box 7407, Washington, DC, 20044; 202-927-2095. Ask for a copy of "Know

Before You Go."

Travellers from other countries should also check on Customs regulations before leaving home.

TAXES

Health Services Tax (Provincial Sales Tax)

New Brunswick has a sales tax on purchased goods and some services. Short-term accommodations and restaurant meals are included under this tax. This tax is to be merged with the federal GST as of April 1997.

Non-residents of New Brunswick may receive a rebate on this tax for goods purchased here and taken out of the province. The rebate must be claimed within 90 days of leaving New Brunswick.

Goods and Services Tax (GST)

There is a federal tax on almost all goods and services sold in Canada (basic groceries are excepted). Non-residents can get a GST rebate on goods purchased for use outside the country provided they are removed from Canada within 60 days of purchase. GST rebates are also available on short-term accommodation (less than 30 days). A rebate cannot be claimed for GST paid on restaurant meals, alcohol, tobacco, car rentals, gas, camping fees, and other services.

GST Rebate forms are available at all provincial tourist information centres and the New Brunswick Duty Free shops at Woodstock (the only instant GST rebate center in Atlantic Canada — summer hours 7 am-11p.m.), Clair and Saint-Leonard. For information on Rebate Guidelines and exemptions please write: Revenue Canada, Customs and Excise, Visitors' Rebate Program, Ottawa, Ontario, K1A 1J5. Or call toll free: 1-800-66-visit (in Canada), 1-613-991-3346 (outside Canada). Take your completed form together with original receipts to participating duty-free shops or mail them to Revenue Canada. Claims may be submitted up to one year from the date of purchase and up to four times a year.

TOURIST INFORMATION CENTRES

The Province maintains Tourist Information Centres at major entry points: Saint-Jacques (Edmundston), Route 2, Trans-Canada Highway (18 km from Edmundston), Woodstock (on Route U.S. 95), St. Stephen, (on highway 1 in centre of town), Aulac, (Route 2 Trans-Canada Highway, 1 km from N.S. border), Campobello (Route 774 across the border from U.S. Route 189), Saint-Leonard (on highway 17 just off Trans-Canada Highway at Saint Leonard) and Campbellton (Salmon Blvd). Other information centres sponsored by municipalities and service clubs are located throughout the province.

Tourist information centres are indicated by a question mark "?" on the New Brunswick Travel Map and along provincial highways.

For more information write to New Brunswick Tourism, P.O. Box 12345, Fredericton, N.B., Canada, E3B 5C3, or telephone toll-free: 1-800-561-0123. From Canada and U.S.A. only; reservations cannot be made.

RESERVATIONS

New Brunswick features a free, in-province accommodation reservations system. It is available at provincial tourist information centres shown at major entry points on the New Brunswick Travel Map. It allows you to make advance reservations directly with hotels, motels, bed and break-fasts, country inns, farm vacations, outfitters and many privately owned campgrounds throughout the province.

GETTING ACQUAINTED

TIME ZONE

New Brunswick falls within the Atlantic Time Zone, which is one hour later than the Eastern Time Zone. Daylight Saving Time, when the clocks are advanced one hour, is in effect from early April until late October. Entering New Brunswick from Maine or Quebec set your watch ahead one hour.

CLIMATE

Weather reports are given in degrees Celsius rather than Fahrenheit. During the summer, days can get quite warm. Temperatures tend to be warmer inland. Temperatures are cooler in the evening.

Average Temperatures:

June	23°C/73°F
July	26°C/79°F
Aug.	25°C/77°F
Sept.	19°C/66°F

Clothing:
May/June: light shirt and pants, sweater or light jacket.
July/August: light summer wear, shorts, t-shirt.
Late September/October: warmer clothing, long pants, sweater, jacket.
November-April: winter clothing, heavy jacket, boots.

METRIC SYSTEM

New Brunswick, like the rest of Canada, has converted to the metric system of weights and measures. Distances and speed limits are based on the kilometre. Gasoline is sold in litres. Temperatures are given in degrees Celsius; snowfall and rainfall amounts in centimetres and millimetres.
Some useful conversions:
   1 kilometre = 0.62 miles
   100 kilometres per hour = 62
      miles per hour
   4 litres of gasoline is roughly
      equal to 1 U.S. gallon
   1 metre = 3.28 feet
   1 centimetre = 0.39 inches
   1 kilogram = 2.2 pounds
   20 degrees Celsius = 68
      degrees Fahrenheit
  To convert degrees Celsius to Fahrenheit, multiply by 2 and add 30 (accurate within 2 degrees).

PUBLIC HOLIDAYS

Banks, schools, and government offices are closed for public holidays, while many other businesses and visitor attractions remain open. New Brunswick public holidays are as follows:
   New Year's Day, January 1
   Good Friday/Easter Monday,
      movable feasts
   Victoria Day (Queen Victoria's
      Birthday), Monday
      preceding May 25
   Canada Day, July 1
   Civic Holiday, Monday
      nearest August 1
   New Brunswick Day, August 1
   Labour Day, First Monday in
      September
   Thanksgiving Day, Second
      Monday in October
   Remembrance Day,
      November 11
   Christmas Day, December 25
   Boxing Day, December 26

STAYING HEALTHY

Medical care in New Brunswick is first-rate, but costly. Visitors are urged to obtain travel health insurance before leaving home. If you require medical services while in New Brunswick, Visitor Information Centres will provide directions to a local hospital.

HOSPITALS/EMERGENCIES

In the event of an emergency visitors should dial 0 or 911. Medical services are listed in the front of telephone directories and are marked by a white H on a green background on road signs.

GETTING AROUND

FERRY SERVICE

On the lower reaches of the St. John River and Kennebecasis River, there are several toll-free ferries in operation. Other free ferries operate between Letete and Deer Island and during the summer between Lameque and Miscou islands. There are toll ferries between New Brunswick and Prince Edward Island, Nova Scotia and Quebec. Within the province, ferries operate from Blacks Harbour to Grand Manan and Deer Island to Campobello. (The latter operates only during the summer.)

HIGHWAYS AND BYWAYS

New Brunswick has an exciting Scenic Drive and alternate routes network including the River Valley Scenic Drive, the Fundy Coastal Drive, the Acadian Coastal Route or the Miramichi River Route. Speed limits are posted in kilometres and permit a maximun of 80 km (50 mph) on provincial highways and 50 km (30 mph) in urban districts unless otherwise indicated. Seat belts are mandatory for drivers and passengers. Children under 5 years of age and under 18 kilograms (40 lbs.) must be in an infant carrier or approved child restraint.

Unleaded and diesel gas are available throughout the province and are sold by the litre. There are 3.78 litres in one U.S. gallon.

Vehicle insurance is compulsory in the province, with a minimum inclusive coverage of $200,000. U.S. motorists are advised to obtain a Canadian Non-Resident Inter-Provincial Motor Vehicle Liability Insurance Card which is accpeted as evidence of financial responsibility anywhere in Canada. It is available only in the United States through U.S. insurance companies. In case of an accident on a highway related to the operation of a motor vehicle, the operator shall offer assistance to the injured person and is required to give his name and address. If total damage amounts to $1000 or over or has caused death or injury to any person, particulars must be reported immediately to the nearest police department.

The driver of a motor vehicle meeting or overtaking a school bus which is displaying red flashing lights shall stop not less than 5 m (16 ft.) from the bus and shall not pass until the bus is again in motion or the lights have stopped flashing.

Trailers are welcome and no entry permit is required. The maximum length allowed for a trailer is 14.46 m (48 ft.); for a trailer plus the towing vehicle, 23 m (75 ft.); and no two- or three-axle motor vehicle may exceed 12.5 m (41 ft.).

LODGINGS

RIVER VALLEY SCENIC DRIVE

Browns Flat
• Riverside Bed and Breakfast,

Beulah Road; (506)468-2820, off-season (813)697-9501. Connie and Tom Greene. Open June 1 to October 31.

Edmundston
• Hotel Republique City Hotels, Canada Road; (506) 739-7321, fax (506) 725-9101 toll free 1-800-654-2000 (E. Canada). Open year round. Licensed Dining room. Licensed lounge bar. Major credit cards.
• Le Fief, 87 Church Street; (506) 735-0400. Sharon and Phil Belanger. Open year round.
• Howard Johnson Hotel and Convention Centre, 100 Rice Street; (506)739-7321, fax (506) 725-9101, toll free 1-800-654-2000. Open year round. Restaurant. Licensed dining room. Major credit cards.

Florenceville
• Beechwood Motel, R R #2; (506) 278-5241. Charlie and Pat Green. Open year round. Restaurant. Major credit cards.

Fredericton
• Carriage House Inn, 230 University Avenue; (506) 452-9924, 1-800-267-6068, fax (506) 458-0799. Joan and Frank Gorham. Open year round. Master Card, Visa.
• Fredericton Inn Limited, 1315 Regent Street; (506) 455-1430. Open year round. Restaurant. Licensed dining room. Licensed lounge bar. Major credit cards.
• Best Western Mactaquac Inn, R R #6; (506) 363-5111, fax (506) 363-3000, toll free 1-800-561-5111. Open year round. Licensed lounge bar. Major credit cards.
• Lord Beaverbrook Hotel, 659 Queen Street; (506) 455-3371, fax (506) 455-1441, toll free 1-800-561-7666. Open year round. Licensed dining room. Licensed lounge bar. Major credit cards.
• Sheraton Inn Fredericton, 225 Woodstock Road; (506) 457-7000, fax (506) 547-4000, toll free 1-800-325-3535. Open year round. Restaurant. Licensed dining room. Licensed lounge bar. Major credit cards.

Gagetown

- Loaves and Calico Country Inn and Café, Tilley Road at Mill Street; (506) 488-3018. Marie Anne Godin. Open April to Christmas and by reservation. Licensed. Visa.
- Steamers Stop Inn, Front Street; (506) 488-2903, fax (506) 488-1116. Pat and Vic Stewart. Open Mother's Day to mid-October. Visa.

Grand Falls

- Best Western – Près du Lac, R R #6; (506) 473-1300, fax (506) 473-5501, toll free 1-800-528-1234. LaForge family. Open year round. Restaurant. Licensed dining room. Licensed lounge bar. Major credit cards.
- Coté Bed and Breakfast, 575 Broadway; (506) 473-1415. Norma and Noel Coté. Open year round. Master Card, Visa.
- Motel Leo Ltd. and La Renaissance Rest., T.C.H. R R #6; (506) 473-2090, fax (506) 473-6614, toll free 1-800-661-0077. Bert and Thérèse Senechal. Open year round. Licensed dining room. Major credit cards.

Hartland

- Campbell's Bed and Breakfast; (506)375-4775. Howard and Rosemary Campbell. Open year round.

Nackawic

- Nackawic Motel Ltd.; (506) 575-8851, (506) 575-8348. Open year round. Master Card, Visa.

New Denmark

- Pederson's Potato Farm, R R #1; (506) 553-6618. Gunnar Pedersen. Open year round.

Perth-Andover

- Demerchant Tourist Home Bed & Breakfast; (506) 273-6152. S. and S. Demerchant. Open year round.
- Perth-Andover Motor Inn; (506) 273-2224. William Linton. Open year round. Licensed dining room. Licensed lounge bar. Major credit cards.

Plaster Rock

- Tobique View Motel and Restaurant; (506) 356-2684, (506) 356-2441, (506) 356-2683. William Linton. Open year round. Licensed dining room. Licensed lounge bar. Major credit cards.

Saint-Jacques

- Ritz Motel and Aquatic Park; (506) 735-4243, fax (506) 739-5334. Licensed dining room. Licensed lounge bar. Amex, Master Card, Visa.
- Ginik's Bed and Breakfast, 241 Principale; (506) 739-6008. Open year round. Master Card, Visa.

St. Léonard

- Daigle's Motel. 68 Bridge Street; (506) 423-6351. Open year round. Restaurant. Licensed dining room. Licensed lounge bar. Major credit cards.

Woodstock

- Auberge Wandlyn Inn; (506) 328-8876, fax (506) 328-4828, toll free 1-800-561-0000 (E. Canada). Open year round. Licensed dining room. Licensed lounge bar. Major credit cards.
- John Gyles Motor Inn Ltd. "German Restaurant," R R #1; (506) 328-6622. Major credit cards. Licensed dining room. Open March to December.
- Sites Motel Hillview Ltd., 827 Main Street; (506) 328-6671. Brent and Mary Dimock. Open year round. Restaurant. Licensed dining room. Licensed lounge bar. Major credit cards.

FUNDY COASTAL DRIVE

Alma

- Captain's Inn, Main Street; (506) 887-2017, fax (506) 887-2074. John and Elsie O'Regan. Open year round.
- Parkland Village Inn, Main Street; (506) 887-2313, Allan and Donna Pittmann. Licensed dining room.

Campobello Island

- Lupine Lodge; (506) 752-2555. Lesley "Lassie" Savage. Open late May to mid-October. Master Card, Visa.

Chance Harbour

- Mariner's Inn, R R #2, Mawhinney

Cove Road; (506) 650-2619, toll free 1-800-463-6062. Matthew and Valerie Mawhinney. Open May to October. Licensed dining room. Master Card, Visa.
- Mountain Ash Manor Bed and Breakfast, R R #2; (506) 659-1100. Betty and Robert "Bud" MacKenzie. Open May through October or by reservation. Visa.

Grand Bay
- Phyl's Beverly Hills Bed and Breakfast, 8 Beverly Hills Drive; (506) 738-2337. Phyllis Finkle. Open year round.

Grand Manan
- Beach Front Cottages, Seal Cove; (506) 662-3115, fax (506) 662-3786. Michael and Tammy Brown. Open year round. Visa.
- The Compass Rose, North Head; (506) 662-8570, (506) 446-5906 (off-season). Cecilia Bowden. Open May 1 to October 31. Visa.
- Manan Island Inn and Spa, North Head; (506) 662-8624. Susan Wilcox-Buchanan. Open year round. Master Card, Visa.
- Marathon Inn (506) 662-8144, North Head; Jim Leslie and Liz Crampton. Open year round. Licensed dining room. Visa, MC.
- McLaughlin's Wharf Inn, Seal Cove; (506) 662-8760, (506) 662-3672. Brenda McLaughlin. Open June through September. Master Card, Visa.
- Shorecrest Lodge, North Head; (506) 662-3216. Mr. and Mrs. Andrew Normandeau. Licensed dining room. Visa.

Hampton
- Bamara Inn, 316 Main Street; (506) 832-9099. Barbara and John McNamara. Open year round. EnRoute, Master Card, Visa.

Hopewell Rocks
- Hopewell Rocks Motel and Country Inn.(506) 734-2975; Open year round. Restaurant. Amex, Master Card, Visa.
- Steeves Family Restaurant – Cottages, R R #1; Bob Steeves. Open May to October. Licensed dining room. Master Card, Visa.

Moncton
- Bonaccord House, 250 Bonaccord; (506) 388-1535, fax (506) 853-7191. Patricia Townsend and Jeremy Martin. Open year round. Visa.
- Crystal Palace Best Western Hotel, 499 Paul Street (Dieppe); (506) 858-8584, fax (506) 5486, toll free 1-800-528-1234. Kris Genthner, G.M. Major Credit Cards. Licensed dining room.
- Hotel Beausejour, Canadian Pacific Hotels and Resorts, 750 Main Street; (506) 854-4344, fax (506) 858-0957, toll free 1-800-441-1414 (Canada and U.S.), toll free 1-800-561-2328 (Maritime Provinces and Quebec). Open year round. Restaurant. Licensed dining room. Licensed lounge bar. Major credit cards.
- Howard Johnson Lodge and Hillside Rest, PO Box 5005, Magnetic Hill; (506) 384-1050, fax (506) 859-6070. Open year round. Licensed dining room. Licensed lounge bar. Major credit cards.

Riverside-Albert
- Florentine Manor, R R #2; (506) 882-2271 (phone and fax), 1-800-665-2271 (Canada). Mary and Cyril Tingley. Open year round. Master Card, Visa.

Rothesay
- Shadow Lawn Country Inn; (506) 847-7539. Patrick and Margaret Gallagher. Open year round. Major credit cards.

Sackville
- Borden's Restaurant and Motel Limited; (506) 536-1066. Open year round.
- The Different Drummer Bed and Breakfast, 82 West Main Street; (506) 536-1291. Georgette and Richard Hanrahan. Open year round. Master Card, Visa.
- Marshlands Inn; (506) 536-0170. Catherine Draper. Open year round. Major credit cards.

Saint John
- The Delta Brunswick Hotel, 39 King Street; (506) 648-1981, fax (506) 658-0914, toll free 1-800-268-1133. Open year round.

Restaurant. Licensed dining room.
Licensed lounge bar. Major credit
cards.
- Dufferin Inn and San Martello
Dining Room, 357 Dufferin Row;
(506) 635-5968, fax (506) 674-
2396. Margaret and Axel Begner.
Open year round. Master Card,
Visa.
- Howard Johnson Hotel, 400 Main
Street; (506) 642-2622. Licensed
Dining Room. Licensed lounge bar.
Major credit cards.
- Inn on the Cove, 1371 Sand Cove
Road; (506) 672-7799, fax (506)
635-5455. Willa and Ross Mavis.
Open year round. Master Card,
Visa.
- Island View Motel, 1726
Manawagonish Road; (506) 672-
1381. Kirit Patel. Open year round.
Master Card, Visa.
- Parkerhouse Inn, 71 Sydney Street;
(506) 652-5054. Pamela Vincent.
Open year round. Licensed. Amex,
Master Card, Visa.
- Saint John Hilton, One Market
Square; (506) 693-8484, fax (506)
657-6610, toll free 1-800-561-
8282. Open year round. Restaurant.
Licensed dining room. Licensed
lounge bar. Major credit cards.

St. Andrews-by-the-Sea
- The Algonquin Resort 1-800-563-
4299; James Frise. Open May
through October. Major credit
cards.
- Chamcook Forest Lodge Bed and
Breakfast, R R #2; (506) 529-4778.
Jenny and Don Menton. Open year
round. Master Card, Visa.
- The Rossmount Inn; (506) 529-
3351. Webber and Alice Burns.
Open May through October. Master
Card, Visa.
- Treadwell Inn, 129 Water Street;
(506) 529-1011, fax (506) 529-
4826. Annette Lacey and Jerry
Mercer. Open May through October
or by reservation. Master Card,
Visa.

St. George
- Granite Town Hotel, 15 Main
Street East, (506) 755-6415, fax
(506) 755-6009. Major credit cards.
Licensed dining room. Open year
round.
- Town House Bed and Breakfast,

Main Street; (506) 755-3476. Pat
and Dan Gillmor. Open May
through October. Visa.

St. Martins
- Quaco Inn, Beach Street; (506)
833-4772. Betty Ann and Bill
Murray. Open year round. Master
Card, Visa.
- St. Martins Country Inn, R R #1; 1-
800-565-5257. Myrna and Albert
LeClair. Open year round. Master
Card, Visa.

St. Stephen
- Blair House, 38 Prince William
Street; (506) 466-2233, fax (506)
466-5636. Betty and Bryan
Whittingham. Open year round.
Master Card, Visa.
- Loon Bay Lodge; (506) 466-1240.
David and Judy Whittingham.
Open May to November. Visa.

Sussex
- Amsterdam Inn, 143 Main Street;
(506) 432-5050, Simone Poirier,
Major credit cards accepted.
- Stark's Hillside Bed and Breakfast,
R R #4. (506) 433-3764, Visa.
- Dutch Valley Heritage Inn,
Waterford Road, R R #4. (506)
433-1339, fax (506) 433-4287.
Vickey and Lawson Bell. Open
year round.

ACADIAN COASTAL DRIVE

Bathurst
- Atlantic Host Inn, Vanier
Boulevard; (506) 548-3335, fax
(506) 548-9769. Open year round.
Restaurant. Licensed dining room.
Licensed lounge bar. Major credit
cards.
- Best Western Danny's Inn and
Conf. Centre, Rte 134; (506) 546-
6621, fax (506) 548-3266, toll free
1-800-528-1234. Robert DeGrace.
Open year round. Restaurant.
Licensed dining room. Licensed
lounge bar. Major credit cards.
- Keddy's Bathurst Hotel and Conv.
Centre, 80 Main Street; (506) 546-
6691, fax (506) 546-0015, toll free
1-800-561-7666. Open year round.
Licensed dining room. Licensed
lounge bar. Major credit cards.

Bouctouche
- Auberge le Vieux Presbytère de Bouctouche 1880, 157 chemin du Couvent; (506) 743-5568, fax (506) 743-5566. Louise Michaud. Open 1 May to 15 October. Master Card, Visa.

Campbellton
- Aylesford Inn, 8 MacMillan Avenue; (506) 759-7672. Richard and Shirley Ayles. Open year round. Licensed dining room. Major credit cards.
- Sanfar Cottages and Country Kettle D.R., Restigouche Drive, Tide Head; (506) 753-4287. Licensed Dining Room. Master Card, Visa.
- Comfort Inn, 3 Sugarloaf Street West; (506) 753-4121, toll free 1-800-228-5150.
- Howard Johnson Hotel, 157 Water Street; (506) 753-4133, toll free 1-800-446-4656.

Caraquet
- Hotel Paulin, 143 Boulevard St. Pierre ouest; (506) 727-9981. Gerard Paulin. Open May to October. Licensed dining room. Master Card, Visa.

Kedgwick
- O Regal Restaurant and Motel Ltée, C.P. 218; (506) 284-2196. René Dubé. Open year round. Restaurant. Major credit cards.

New Mills
- Bonaventure Lodge, Highway 11; (506) 237-2134. Open from 1 July to 31 August, daily 8 am to 10 p.m.. Shorter hours in the spring and fall. Licensed. Master Card, Visa.

Shediac
- Chez Françoise, (506) 532-4233. Jacques and Helene Cadieux Johanny. Open May through December. Major credit cards.
- Four Seas Restaurant and Motel, 762 Main Street; (506) 532-2585. Open year round. Restaurant. Licensed dining room. Licensed lounge bar. Major credit cards.

Shippagan
- Maison Touristique Mallet; R R #2; (506) 336-4167. Alice Mallet. Year round.

Tracadie-Sheila
- Motel Boudreau Ltée, C.P. 1449; (506) 395-2244, fax (506) 395-6868, toll free 1-800-563-2242. Donald Boudreau. Open year round. Licensed dining room. Licensed lounge bar. Major credit cards.

MIRAMICHI RIVER ROUTE

Chatham-Miramichi
- Black Brook Cabin Rentals; (506) 778-2498. Debbie Comeau. Open year round.

Doaktown
- O'Donnell's Cottages on the Miramichi, 439 Storeytown Road; (506) 365-7924. Valerie and Jackie O'Donnell. Open April 15 to October 1.

Millerton
- Betts Homestead, R R #1; (506) 622-2511, (506) 622-5157. Open year round. Visa.

Newcastle-Miramichi
- Auberge Wandlyn Inn, 365 Water Street; (506) 622-3870, fax (506) 622-3250, toll free 1-800-561-0000 (E. Canada). Open year round. Licensed dining room. Licensed lounge bar. Major credit cards.
- The Wharf Inn, 1 Jane Street; (506) 622-0302, fax (506) 622-0354, toll free 1-800-561-2111. Claire McKenna-Jean. Open year round. Restaurant. Licensed dining room. Licensed lounge bar. Major credit cards.

Renous
- Sunshine Motel and Restaurant, R R #1; (506) 622-2477. Open year round. Licensed dining room. Major credit cards.

DINING

RIVER VALLEY SCENIC DRIVE

Edmundston
- Steak and Seafood Paradise, 174 Victoria Street, (506) 739-7822; Licensed.

Fredericton

- Bruno, Sheraton Inn, Woodstock Road. (506) 457-7000. 6:30 am-11 pm daily.
- City Motel, The Lobster Hut, 1216 Regent Street; (506) 450-9900. Open all day every day. Licensed. Amex, Master Card, Visa.
- Dimitri's, 349 King Street; (506) 452-8882, Yvon Durand. Open all day every day. Licensed. Amex, Master Card, Visa.
- The Hilltop Pub, 152 Prospect Street E; (506) 458-9057, toll free 1-800-561-7666. Open all day every day. Licensed. Amex, Master Card, Visa.
- Lord Beaverbrook Hotel, 659 Queen Street; (506) 455-3371, toll free 1-800-561-7666. Open all day every day. Licensed. Amex, Master Card, Visa.
- The Lunar Rogue, 625 King Street; (506) 450-2065. Closed Sunday. Licensed. Amex, Master Card, Visa.
- Sheraton Inn, Fredericton, 225 Woodstock Road; (506) 457-7000, toll free 1-800-267-6068.
- Fredericton Inn, 1315 Regent Street; (506) 455-1430, toll free 1-800-561-8777.
- Puzzles, 247 Main Street, on the north side; (506) 450-4108. Opens at 4 pm on Sunday and closes at 3 on Monday. Licensed. Amex, Master Card, Visa.

Gagetown

- Loaves and Calico, Tilley Road at Mill Street; (506) 488-3018. Marie Anne Godin. Open Monday to Saturday 10 am to 6 pm; Sunday noon to 8 pm from early April until late November. Licensed. Visa.
- Steamers Stop Inn, Front Street; (506) 488-2903, fax (506) 488-1116. Pat and Vic Stewart. Open from Mother's Day to mid-October. Visa.

Hartland

- Ja-Sa-Lee, Highway 2; (506) 375-4419. Open winter and summer, Monday to Friday 7 am to 2 pm, 5 pm to 8 pm. Licensed. Master Card and Visa.

Perth-Andover

- Maximilian, 99 Gore Street E;

(613) 267-2536. Open Monday to Friday 11:30 am to 2 pm, 5 pm to 9 pm, Saturday and Sunday 5 pm to 9 pm from June 1 until September 30, closed on Monday in winter. Licensed. Master Card, Visa.

Plaster Rock

- Tobique View Motel; (506) 356-2683. Open all day every day (until 10 pm in summer, 8 pm in winter). Licensed. All cards.

Stanley

- Cornish Corner Inn; turn off highway 8 from Fredericton at 107 and allow 40 minutes for the trip; (506) 367-2239. Sheelagh Wagener. Open from 1 May to 31 March, daily 11 am to 9 pm. Licensed. Amex, Master Card, Visa.

FUNDY COASTAL DRIVE

Aulac

- Drury Lane Steak House, see Acadian Coastal Route.

Dorchester

- Bell Inn, Highway 106; (506) 379-2580. David McAllister. Open March 1 to December 31, Tuesday to Sunday 10 am to 7 pm. Not licensed. No credit cards.

Grand Manan

- The Compass Rose, North Head; (506) 662-8570. Cecilia Bowden. Open May through October, Monday to Saturday 8 am to 10 am, noon to 2 pm, 3 pm to 4 pm, 6 pm to 8.30 pm, Sunday 8 am to 10 am, noon to 2 pm, 3 pm to 4 pm. Not licensed. Visa.
- McLaughlin's Wharf Inn, Seal Cove; (506) 662-8760, (506) 662-3672. Brenda McLaughlin. Open June through September. EnRoute, Master Card, Visa.

Hampton

- Bamara Inn, 316 Main Street; (506) 832-9099. Barbara and John McNamara. Open year round. EnRoute, Master Card, Visa.

Moncton

- Gaston's Restaurant, 44 rue Main Street; (506) 858-8998. Gaston

Frigault. Open year round. Licensed. Major credit cards.
- L'Auberge, Hotel Beausejour, 750 rue Main Street; (506) 854-4344. Open daily 7 am to 10:30 pm. Licensed. Amex, Master Card, Visa.

Petitcodiac
- Two Brothers, 71 Main Street; (506) 756-8111. Roger and Dana Steeves. Open daily 5:30 pm to 10 pm. Licensed. Amex, Master Card, Visa.

Rothesay
- Shadow Lawn Country Inn, 3180 Rothesay Road; (506) 847-7539. Patrick and Margaret Gallagher. Open year round. Major credit cards.

Sackville
- Marshlands Inn, 73 Bridge Street; (506) 536-0170. Catherine Draper. Open year round, daily 7 am to 10 am, 11:30 am to 2 pm, 5:30 pm to 8:30 pm. Licensed. Major credit cards.

Saint John
- Boyce's Gallery, 38 Coburg Street; (506) 632-1290. Rhoda Boyce. Open 11 am to 4 pm six days a week. Not licensed. Visa.
- Dufferin Inn and San Martello Dining Room, 357 Dufferin Row; (506) 635-5968, fax (506) 674-2396. Margaret and Axel Begner. Open year round. Master Card, Visa.
- La Belle Vie, 325 Lancaster Avenue; (506) 635-1155. Patrick Masset. Open Monday to Friday 11 am to 2 pm, 5 pm to 9:30 pm, Saturday and Sunday 5 pm to 9:30 pm. Licensed. Master Card, Visa.
- Parkerhouse Inn, 71 Sydney Street; (506) 652-5054. Pamela Vincent. Open year round. Licensed. Amex, Master Card, Visa.
- The Whale of a Café, City Market, 47 Charlotte Street; (506) 632-1900. Open all day every day except Sunday. Not licensed. No credit cards.

St. Andrews-by-the-Sea
- L'Europe, 48 King Street; (506) 529-3818. Anita Ludwig. Open early May to late September,

Tuesday to Saturday 6 pm to 11 pm Licensed. Visa.
- Passamaquoddy Room, Algonquin Hotel; (506) 529-8823. Open June 1 to September 30, Monday to Saturday noon to 2 pm, 6 pm to 9 pm, Sunday 11.30 am to 3 pm, 6 pm to 9 pm. Licensed. All cards.
- Rossmount Inn, Highway 127; (506) 529-3351. Webber and Alice Burns. Open June 1 to October 31, daily 6:30 pm to 9 pm. Licensed. Master Card, Visa.

St. Martins
- Quaco Inn, Beach Street; (506) 833-4772. Katherine Landry. Open year round. Licensed. Master Card, Visa.
- St. Martins Country Inn, R R #1; 1-800-565-5257. Myrna and Albert LeClair. Open year round. Master Card, Visa.

St. Stephen
- Loon Bay Lodge; (506) 466-1240. David and Judy Whittingham. Open May to November. Visa.

Sussex
- Broadway Café, 73 Broadway Street; (506) 433-5414. Judith and Peter Williams. Open Monday to Thursday 9 am to 3 pm, Friday 9 am to 9 pm, Saturday 10 am to 9 pm. Licensed for beer and wine only. Amex, Master Card, Visa.

ACADIAN COASTAL DRIVE

Aulac
- Drury Lane Steak House; (506) 536-1252. Sharon Meldrum. Open mid-May to mid-October, open for lunch and dinner. Major credit cards.

Bouctouche
- Auberge le Vieux Presbytère de Bouctouche 1880, 157 Chemin du Coubent; (506) 743-5568. Louise Michaud. Open May to October. Licensed. Master Card, Visa.

Campbellton
- Aylesford Inn, 8 MacMillan Avenue; (506) 759-7672. Richard and Shirley Ayles. Open year round. Major credit cards.

Caraquet
- Hotel Paulin, 143 boulevard St.-Pierre Ouest; (506) 727-3165, fax (506) 727-3300. Gerard Paulin. Open May to October, Monday to Friday 11:30 am to 2 pm, 5:30 pm to 9 pm. Licensed. Master Card, Visa.
- La Poissonnière Restaurant, see Grand-Anse.

Chatham
- The Cunard, see Chatham, Miramichi River Route.

Grand-Anse
- La Poissonnière Restaurant, 484 Acadie Street; (506) 732-2000. Richard Chiasson. Open Fathers' Day to September. Major credit cards.

Inkerman
- The Quai du Capitaine, Highway 113; (506) 336-9697. Open daily from 4 pm to 11 pm. Licensed. Most credit cards.

New Mills
- Bonaventure Lodge, Highway 11; (506) 237-2134. Open from July 1 to August 31, daily 8 am to 10 pm. Shorter hours in the spring and fall. Licensed. Master Card, Visa.

Shediac
- Chez Françoise, 93 Main Street; (506) 532-4233. Jacques and Hélène Cadieux Johanny. Open May through December. Major credit cards.

Shippagan
- Lobster Deck, 118 Main Street; (506) 532-8737. Fully licensed. Open May to October.
- The Quai du Capitaine, see Inkerman, Acadian Coastal Route.

MIRAMICHI RIVER ROUTE

Chatham-Mirimichi
- The Cunard, 32 Cunard Street; (506) 773-7107. Open Monday to Friday 11 am to midnight, Saturday noon to midnight, Sunday 11 am to 10 pm. Licensed. Master Card, Visa.

ATTRACTIONS

RIVER VALLEY SCENIC DRIVE

Fredericton
- Beaverbrook Art Gallery. Open July 1 to Labour Day, Mon-Fri 9 am-6 pm, Sat-Sun 10 am-5 pm; Sept-June, Tues-Fri 9 am-5 pm, Sat 10 am-5 pm, Sun 12 pm-5 pm. Admission: adults $3. Tours are self-guided. Photography not permitted. Phone (506) 458-8545; 458-8546
- Christ Church Cathedral. Open year round daily 9 am-5 pm, except Sunday mornings. Free admission. Tours are self-guided. Information booklets are available. Photography permitted. Phone (506) 450-8500.
- Guardhouse. Open mid-June to Labour Day, weekdays 10 am-6 pm. Free admission. Tours are guided by a costumed soldier of the old British 15th Regiment. Photography permitted. Phone (506)453-3747.
- Legislative Assembly Building. Open June-Labour Day, daily 9 am-8 pm; rest of the year, Mon-Fri 9 am-4 pm. Free admission. All tours are guided. Large groups should make reservations. Phone (506) 453-2527.
- York-Sunbury Museum. Open: May 1 to Labour Day, Monday to Saturday 10:00 am to 6:00 pm, July and August also Tuesday and Thursday 10:00 am to 9:00 pm and Sunday 12:00 pm to 6:00 pm Labour Day to mid-October, Monday to Friday 9:00 am to 5:00 pm, Saturday 12:00 pm to 4:00 pm Mid-October to April, Monday, Wednesday, and Friday 11:00 am to 3:00 pm. Admission is $2 per adult. Tours are self-guided. Photography not permitted. Phone: (506) 455-6041.

Gagetown
- Loomcrofters. Open May 1 to October 31, Monday to Saturday 10:00 am to 5:00 pm, Sunday 2:00 pm to 5:00 pm For special appointments, call Enid Inch at (506) 488-2400. Free admission. Tours are self-guided, but the weavers will gladly answer any questions. Photography

permitted. To get there from Fredericton, take N.B. 102 south for about 64 km (40 mi.). As the 102 turns right near Gagetown, continue straight into town. Turn right after three blocks on Tilley Road, which later becomes Loomcroft Lane. Pass the Gagetown School and keep left until the road ends at a small cedar-shingled house. This is the loomcrofters' studio.

- Sir Leonard Tilley House. Open: Mid-June to mid-September, daily 10:00 am to 5:00 pm; mid-September to Canadian Thanksgiving, weekends only. Admission: $1.00 per adult. All tours are guided. Photography: permitted. Phone: (506) 488-2966. To get there from the Loomcrofters' studio, turn back onto Loomcroft Lane. Turn right on Mill Road and follow it to a T-junction facing Greig Pottery store and workshop. Turn left onto Front Street. Tilley House Museum is located on the left just before the Anglican Church and cemetery.

Grand Falls

- The Gorge. Accessible year round. Lighting is also provided throughout the year from 10:00 pm to 12:00 pm; the pathway Lovers' Lane opposite the visitor centre is lighted until 1 am. La Rochelle nearby is a place offering access to the Wells in Rocks. Both La Rochelle and the Malabeam Visitor Centre are open from 9 am to 9 pm from the end of May to the beginning of September. Admission free at the gorge, the Wells in Rocks are accessible through La Rochelle at a charge of $2.00 per adult to a maximum of $5.00 per family. All tours are self-guided. Information is readily available at the Malabeam Reception Centre. Photography permitted. Phone: (506) 473-6013. To get there from the north, exit the Trans-Canada Highway (#2) at exit 75 and follow the road to a major intersection with a traffic light. Just before reaching the intersection, the Malabeam Visitor Centre is located on the right. From the south, exit the Trans-Canada Highway (#2) at Grand Falls Portage, and follow

N.B. 130 for a while. In the town of Grand Falls, the road makes a sharp right turn and becomes Broadway. Continue straight, cross the Turcotte Bridge and immediately turn left. The Malabeam Visitor Centre and Museum is on the left side of the road.

- Grand Falls Museum Open mid-June to September 1, Monday to Friday 9:00 am to 10:00 pm, Saturday and Sunday 2:00 pm to 5:00 pm. Admission free. Guided tour available. Photography permitted. Phone: (506) 473-5265 To get there from the Malabeam Visitor Centre, cross the Turcotte Bridge, continue on Broadway, and turn left onto Church Street, follow it for one block and turn left again onto Sheriff Street. The museum is located in the basement of the public library on the corner of Church and Sheriff Streets.

Hartland

- Hartland Bridge. The village of Hartland is located a short distance off the Trans-Canada Highway about 20 minutes north of Woodstock.

Kings Landing

- Kings Landing Historical Settlement. Open first Saturday in June to Canadian Thanksgiving, 10:00 am to 5:00 pm; July & August, 10:00 am to 6:00 pm Admission is $8.00 per adult. Annual passes and family rates are available. Tours are self-guided. Photography permitted. The settlement is located near the Trans-Canada Highway about 35 km (22 mi.) west of Fredericton at exit #250. For more information call (506) 363-5090.

New Denmark

- New Denmark Museum. Founders' Day is on June 19. The celebration takes place on June 19 or the first Sunday following. The museum is open July 1 to Labour Day, daily from 9:00 am to 5:00 pm. Admission to the museum and the dances is free. Guides are available at the museum. Photography permitted at the museum and at the dances. Phone (506) 553-6724. To get there, leave the Trans-Canada Highway at Grand Falls and take N.B. 108 east for about 9 km (5.6 mi.). Turn right onto Klokkedahl Hill. This road first turns sharply to the left and then ascends steeply. Proceed through a stop sign and pass two churches on opposite sides of the road. They are the Lutheran St. Peter's on the right and the Anglican St. Ansgar's on the left. Continue on the main road. The stage for the dances, the museum, and Immigrant House are all located on the left just before highway N.B. 380 turns off to the left.

Oromocto
• CFB Gagetown Military Museum. Open July and August, Monday to Friday, 9:00 am to 5:00 pm, weekends 12:00 pm to 5:00 pm; September to June, Monday to Friday 8:30 am to 12:00 pm, 1:00 pm to 4:00 pm. Admission free. A guide is available for questions. Photography permitted. Phone: (506) 422-2630. To get there from Fredericton, take N.B. 7 to Oromocto. Exit at Oromocto-Gagetown and continue on N.B. 102 south. Pass a tank and Oromocto High School and turn right at a traffic light onto Broad Road. Turn left onto St. Lawrence Avenue, enter the main gate and follow the green signs to the museum in building A5.

Plaster Rock
• Fraser Inc. lumber mill. Tours are conducted on Tuesdays and Thursdays year round. If at all possible, visitors should give at least one day's notice by calling (506) 356-4117. Admission free. All tours are guided. This is a working mill, so hard hats, provided by the company, must be worn and caution must be exercised at all times. Each tour takes about 1 to 1 1/2 hours. Photography permitted. In Plaster Rock, take N.B. 108, cross the Tobique River bridge, and turn left at a Fraser Inc. sign. Pass by a gas station and stop at the gate. Tours start at the office next to the gate.

Saint-Jacques
• Automobile Museum. Open June 15 to Labour Day, 8:00 am to 8:00 pm. Admission is $2.50 per adult. The tours are self-guided. Photography permitted. Phone: (506) 735-8769. Follow the Trans-Canada Highway (#2) west towards Quebec. Pass by Edmundston and exit near the town of Saint-Jacques. Follow the signs to the Jardins de la République Provincial Park.
• New Brunswick Botanical Garden. Open June to Labour Day, 8:30 am to 9:30 pm daily; Labour Day to mid-October 9:00 am to 7:30 pm daily. Admission $4.50. Tours are self-guided; guided services are available upon request. Photography permitted. Phone: (506) 739-6335.

St. Léonard
• Madawaska Weavers Open Monday to Friday 9:00 am to 12:00 pm and 1:00 pm to 5:00 pm year round. Admission free. Photography permitted. Phone: (506) 423-6341 From the Trans-Canada Highway, take exit #58 at St. Léonard and follow rue Principale Street for .8 km (.5 mi.) into town. At a Stop sign, turn left onto St. Jean. Madawaska Weavers is the second house on the left.

Upper Woodstock
• Old Carleton County Courthouse. Open end of June to Labour Day, 9:30 am to 8:00 pm For other times, call 328-9706. Admission free. Donations are accepted. Guided tours are available. Photography permitted. From the town of Woodstock, take N.B. 103 north. Turn left onto N.B. 560. The courthouse is a short distance away on the left. The large white building cannot be missed.
• Wesleyan Church. Open in summer on weekday mornings from 9:00 am to 12:00 pm. Admission free. No guided tours. Photography permitted.
• Courthouse. Open year round on weekdays, 8:30 am to 5:00 pm.

FUNDY COASTAL DRIVE

Albert County

- Museum and Courthouse. Open June 15 to September 15 open daily from 10:00 am to 6:00 pm. Admission: $1.50 per adult. All tours are self-guided. Photography permitted. No flash photography is allowed in a small room with light-sensitive material. Phone: (506) 734-2003. From Moncton's Albert Bridge, follow N.B. 114 for about 32 km (20 mi.) to the Albert County Museum, located on the right hand side of the road. The famous Hopewell Rocks are just 3 km (2 mi.) further down the road.

Campobello

- Roosevelt Cottage. Open mid-May to end of September, daily 9:00 am to 5:00 pm (EDT) or 10:00 am to 6:00 pm (ADT). Admission free. Guides are available in both buildings. Photography permitted. Cross the border at St. Stephen to Calais and drive south on #1 towards Machias. At Whiting, turn left onto #189 to Lubec. Cross the International Bridge onto Campobello Island. The cottages are located a short distance beyond the customs house on the left. Note that all travellers must carry appropriate identification in order to enter the U.S. An alternate route during the summer months would be to take the ferry from Deer Island directly to Campobello Island or to Eastport, Maine. For details about the schedule, call N.B. tourism at 1-800-442-4442 (within New Brunswick) or 1-800-561-0123 (from anywhere else in Canada and the U.S.).

Chamcook

- Atlantic Salmon Centre. Open spring to fall, daily 10:00 am to 6:00 pm. Admission: $1 per adult. A guide is available for questions. Photography permitted. Located in Chamcook on N.B. 127 en route to St. Andrews.

Dorchester

- Beechkirk Collection (Textile Museum). Open June 1 to Labour Day, 1:00 pm to 5:00 pm; all other days 10:00 am to 5:00 pm Closed on Mondays. Admission $1. Guided tours available throughout the day. Photography permitted. From Moncton follow N.B. 106 to the town of Dorchester. The Beechkirk Collection is housed in St. James Presbyterian Church on the right side of the road.
- Keillor House Museum. Open June 1 to September 15, Sundays 1:00 pm to 5:00 pm; all other days 10:00 am to 5:00 pm. Closed on Mondays. Admission: $1. All tours are guided. Photography prohibited inside the house. Phone: (506) 379-6633; 379-2205 during off season. From Moncton, take N.B. 106 to the town of Dorchester. Keillor House is located a short distance beyond St. James Church on the left, next to the penitentiary.

Grand Manan

- Grand Manan Ferry. Cost: $24.60 per vehicle plus $8.20 per adult. Phone: (506) 662-3606; 662-3724. Year round ferry service between Blacks Harbour on the mainland and North Head on Grand Manan. There are three ferries daily in the off-season and six ferries in the summer. The first ferry from Blacks Harbour leaves at 9:30 am (7:30 am in the summer), and the last ferry departs the island at 5:30 pm throughout the year. The ferries are on time and do not wait! The crossing takes about 1– 1 1/2 hours.
- Grand Manan Museum. Open mid-June to September 30, Monday to Saturday 10:30 am to 4:30 pm, Sundays 1:00 pm to 5:00 pm. Admission: $1 per adult. Photography permitted. Phone: (506) 662-3524

Hampton

- Kings County Museum. Open June 15 to mid-September, Monday to Saturday 10:00 am to 5:00 pm, Sunday 2:00 pm to 5:00 pm. Admission: Adults $1. Tours in the old jail are guided. Photography permitted. Phone: (506) 832-6008. The community of Hampton is located near N.B. 1 approximately halfway between Sussex and Saint John. From Saint John, turn off

N.B. 1 and follow N.B. 121 — here called Main Street — to a junction where N.B. 121 turns off to the left. The courthouse and museum are located on the far left of the junction. Parking is available behind the courthouse.

Hillsborough

- Hillsborough Historic Train. One-hour train rides are offered every Sunday, from mid-June to Labour Day. In addition, a small museum is open seven days a week during the season. Admission fee. Charters available on request. Dinner excursions are available once a month as are charters. For more information, call (506) 734-3195 between 8:00 am and 4:30 pm. Photography permitted. From the Trans-Canada Highway east of Sussex, turn southeast onto N.B. 114. Continue through Fundy National Park, and the towns of Alma, Riverside Albert, to Hillsborough. The train station is on the right side of the road. Alternatively, you can reach Hillsborough on N.B. 114 from Moncton. The distance from Moncton is approximately 24 km (15 mi.).
- William Henry Steeves House. Open July to Labour Day, 10:00 am to 6:00 pm during the season. Admission: $1.75 per adult. All tours are guided. Photography permitted. Phone: (506) 734-3102. Visitors who approach the town from Fundy National Park, pass the railroad station and turn onto Mill Street, the next small street on the right. Steeves House is located at the end of the street across from St. Mary's Anglican Church.

Hopewell Rocks

- Open June 15 to Labour Day, 8:00 am to 5:00 pm At other times, the gate may be closed, but you can park in front of the gate and walk the short distance to the cliffs. For tide schedule call N.B. Tourism at 1-800-442-4442. Admission: $2.50 per car in the summer during regular business hours (see above). Tours are self-guided. A leaflet is available at the viewpoint. Photography permitted. From

Moncton, follow N.B. 114 south along the bay. The Rocks are located on the left side of the road. They are well advertised and cannot be missed.

Mary's Point

- Shepody National Wildlife Area: bird migration. The fall migration can be viewed best between the end of July and mid-August a couple of hours before and after high tide. The tidal schedule is available from N.B. Tourism by calling 1-800-561-0123 (from Canada and the U.S.) or 1-800-442-4442 from within New Brunswick. In addition, a small museum is open during July and August. Admission free. Photography recommended. Bring binoculars. To reach Mary's Point, drive along N.B. 114 from Sussex to Alma, a small former shipbuilding town with tourist facilities located at the southeastern entrance of Fundy National Park. Continue through town, then turn right onto N.B. 915 and follow this road for 25.4 km (15.8 mi.). A dirt road to the right leads 3.2 km (2 mi.) to Mary's Point, which is part of the Shepody National Wildlife Area. Parking space is on the right.

Moncton

The city walking tour outlined is approximately 3.3 km (2 mi.) long.
- Magnetic Hill. Open mid-May to mid-October, 10:00 am to 5:00 pm, July and August 8:00 am to 9:00 pm. Admission free.
- The Moncton Museum & Free Meeting House. Open Monday to Saturday 10:00 am to 4:30 pm, Sunday 1:00 pm to 4:30 pm Admission free. All tours are self-guided. Photography permitted, but no flash photography in the museum. Phone: (506) 856-4383
- Thomas Williams House. Open July and August, Monday to Saturday 10:00 am to 6:00 pm, Sunday 1:00 pm to 6:00 pm; the same in June, but closed Mondays. May and September, Monday, Wednesday and Friday 11:00 am. to 3:00 pm. Admission free. Donations are suggested. All tours are guided. Photography permitted. Phone: (506) 857-0590.

Peticodiac

- Delia's Doll Museum. Open June 15 to September 15, 11:00 am to 7:00 pm or by appointment. Admission: $2.50 per adult. Photography permitted Phone: (506) 756-2254. Museum plus second-hand shop, dolls and clothes.

Sackville

- Atlantic Waterfowl Celebration. Second weekend in August. Admission free. Tickets for individual events are also available. Admission to the Live Bait Theatre is $8. Inquiries may be directed to: Atlantic Waterfowl Celebration, c/o Executive Director, P.O. Box 1078E Sackville, N.B. E0A 3C0. For more information, call (506)364-8080.
- The Harness Shop Open Monday to Friday 8:00 am to 5:00 pm, Saturday 9:00 am to 5:00 pm, year round. Admission free. Phone: (506) 536-0642.

St. Andrews

- County Courthouse and Gaol. Open July and August, Monday to Saturday 9:30 am to 12:00 am, 1:00 pm to 4:30 pm. The County Courthouse is located in the centre of St. Andrews on Frederick and Parr Streets.
- Huntsman Marine Science Centre & Aquarium/Museum. Open July and August, daily 10:00 am to 6:00 pm; May to June as well as September to Canadian Thanksgiving, 10:00 am to 4:30 pm daily. Feeding of the seals is conducted daily at 11:00 am and 4:00 pm. Admission: $4 per adult. Explanations are given at feeding time at 11:00 am and 4:30 pm. Otherwise, the tour is self-guided. Photography permitted. Phone: (506) 529-1202. Drive west on Water Street and continue on this road, later called Brandy Cove Road. Follow the signs to the Huntsman Aquarium/ Museum.
- Ross Memorial Museum Open late May to early October, Monday to Saturday 10:00 am to 4:30 pm; July to September also Sundays 1:30 pm to 4:30 pm. Admission free. Guides are available for questions.

Photography not permitted inside. Phone: (506) 529-1824. Located in the centre of St. Andrews on the corner of King and Montague.
- Sheriff Andrew's House. Open July to late September, Monday to Saturday 9:30 am. to 4:30 pm, Sunday, 1:00 pm to 4:30 pm. Admission free. Guides are available for questions. Photography permitted. Phone: (506) 529-5080 Located in the centre of St. Andrews at 63 King Street.

Saint John

- Carleton Martello Tower. Open June 1 to October 15, daily 9:00 am to 5:00 pm. Admission free. Guides are available for questions. Photography permitted. Phone: (506) 636-4011; 851-3083 during off season. Enter the city of Saint John on highway N.B. 1 and take exit #107 towards Reversing Falls. Turn left at the Stop sign, and right at the traffic light. Cross the railroad tracks and turn right onto Lancaster Avenue. Turn right at a fork, and right again at the end of the street. The tower is on the right-hand side.
- Centenary-Queen Square United Church. Open June to the end of September, Monday to Friday, 9:00 am to 12:00 am. Guided tours available in July and August. Photography permitted. Phone: (506) 634-8288
- Saint John Firefighters' Museum. Open July to August, Monday to Friday 10:00 am to 4:00 pm. Guided tours available if desired. Admission free. Photography permitted. Phone: (506) 663-1840
- Fort Howe Lookout. Enter the city on N.B. 1 and take exit #107 towards Reversing Falls. Turn left at the Stop sign and right at the traffic light. Cross the railroad tracks and continue straight ahead at a junction. Pass Reversing Falls, cross the bridge and continue straight ahead for about 1 km (.6 mi.) to an underpass, followed immediately by a traffic light and St. Luke Church (light blue) on the left. Continue straight on Lansdowne, turn right on Metcalfe Street and keep left as it forks. The

park is a short distance ahead on your right. Phone: (506) 658-2990

- Loyalist House. Open mid-June to September, Monday to Saturday 10:00 am to 5:00 pm; in July & August also Sunday 1:00 pm to 5:00 pm. Guided tours available upon request. Admission: $2 per adult. Photography permitted. Phone: (506) 652-3590

- NBTel and Telephone Pioneers Museum. Open mid-June to mid-September, Monday to Friday 10:00 am to 4:00 pm. Tours for larger groups can be arranged outside these times. Guided tours available upon request. Admission free. Photography permitted. Phone: (506) 694-2973

- New Brunswick Museum. Open year round, Monday to Wednesday 9:00 am to 6:00 p.m, Thursday to Friday 9:00 am to 9:00 pm, Saturday 9:00 am to 6:00 pm; Sunday 12:00 pm to 5:00 pm. Admission: $2.14 per adult. Tours are self-guided. Photography not permitted. Phone: (506) 643-2300, (506) 643-2360. Enter the city on N.B. 1 and take exit #107 towards Reversing Falls. Turn left at the stop sign and right at the traffic light. Cross the railroad tracks and continue straight ahead at a junction. Pass Reversing Falls, pass a bridge and turn left onto Douglas Avenue. Follow the street for about 1 km (.6 mi.). The museum is on the left side of the street. The museum moves to Market Square in summer 1996.

- New Brunswick Botanical Garden: 7 hectares (18 acres) with over 50,000 plants, small waterfall, classical music, giftshop, snackbar.

- Partridge Island and Museum. Tours May to October. Call (506) 635-0782. Special interest tours are also offered as well as chartered tours. Admission: $10 per adult. All tours are guided. Photography permitted. The boat (capacity 40) leaves from the Market Slip wharf next to the Hilton International.

- Reversing Falls. Open mid-May to mid-June and Labour Day to Canadian Thanksgiving, daily 8:00 am to 7:00 pm; mid-June to Labour Day, daily 8:00 am to 9:00 pm. Admission free. The video is shown every hour on the hour for $1.25 per adult. Information is available in the visitor centre and shop. Photography permitted. Enter the city on highway N.B. 1 and take exit #107 towards Reversing Falls. Turn left at the Stop sign and right at the traffic light. Cross the railroad tracks and continue straight ahead at a junction. The visitor centre and ample parking are found on the right side of the street.

- Saint John Jewish Historical Museum. Open end of May to end of September, Monday to Friday 10 am to 4 pm; July and August also Sunday 1:00 pm to 4:00 pm. During the rest of the year, tours are by appointment only. The minimum group size is 10. All tours are guided. Admission free. Photography permitted. Phone: (506) 633-1833

- St. John's Stone Church. Open June to the end of September, Monday to Friday 9:00 am to 4:30 pm. Guided tours: available in July and August. Self-guided tours during June and September. Photography permitted.

- Saint John: Trinity Church Opening Hours: Daily 9:00 am to 3:30 pm. No guides. Photography permitted.

St. Stephen
- Charlotte County Museum. Open June through August, Monday to Saturday 9:30 am to 4:30 pm. Admission free. Guided Tours. Photography permitted. Entering St. Stephen from N.B. 1 or N.B. 3, follow King Street to its end at the wharf. Turn right and follow Milltown Boulevard for about 1.6 km (1 mi.). The museum is on the right side of the road.

- Ganong Factory Tours. Factory tours are available only during a few days of the Chocolate Festival. Prior reservations are mandatory. Call the Chocolate hotline at (506) 465-5616. Admission: $2. All tours are guided. Photography not allowed inside the building. Approaching St. Stephen on N.B. 1 or N.B. 3, continue straight through the traffic circle onto King Street and take the next left onto Chocolate Drive. It leads directly to the factory.

Sussex

- Agricultural Museum of New Brunswick. Open June 15 to mid-October, daily 10:00 am to 5:00 pm, Sundays 12:00 am to 5:00 pm. Admission: $2 for adults. Guided tours available if desired. Photography permitted. Phone: (506) 433-6799. From the Trans-Canada Highway, enter town on Main Street, cross the railroad tracks, and continue straight. As you leave town, turn left onto Leonard Drive. The museum is located not far beyond the bridge on the left side of the road. There are signs, but the most prominent landmark is a red caboose next to the museum.
- Co-op Cattle Auction. The auction takes place every Wednesday morning. It starts between 10:00 am and 11:00 am Visitors are welcome. Photography permitted. How to get there: in Sussex, follow Main Street just across the railroad tracks and turn right onto Park Street which parallels the tracks. Follow it for 1.6 km (1 mi.). The auction barn is on the right side of the street.

ACADIAN COASTAL DRIVE

Aulac

- Fort Beauséjour. Open daily 9:00 am to 5:00 pm from June 1 to October 15. Admission free. Photography permitted everywhere. Phone: (506) 536-0720. Take N.B. 2, the Trans-Canada Highway, east out of Sackville. In Aulac, not far from the visitor centre next to an Esso gas station on the left, turn right. Follow that small road for about 1.6 km (1 mi.) to its end.

Bouctouche

- Kent County Museum (and Old Convent). Open late June to Labour Day, Monday to Saturday 9:00 am to 5:30 pm, Sundays 12:00 pm to 6:00 pm. Admission: $3 per adult. The tour is guided. Photography permitted. Phone: (506) 743-5005. In Bouctouche, take N.B. 475 for a short distance. The museum/convent is located on the left side of the road.
- Le Pays de la Sagouine Theme Park. Open mid-June to Labour Day daily 10:00 am to 8:00 pm, September 10:00 am to 6:00 pm. Admission: $6.00 per adult. All tours are self-guided. Photography permitted. Phone: (506) 743-1400. In Bouctouche, follow the signs to "Le Pays."

Campbellton

- Sugarloaf Mountain. The park is open year round. Admission free. Take N.B. 11 to Campbellton, and follow the signs to Sugarloaf Provincial Park.

Caraquet

- Acadian Historical Village, near Caraquet. Open mid-June to the end of August, 10:00 am to 6:00 pm; August 31 to September 20, 10:00 am to 5:00 pm. Admission: $8.00 per adult. All tours are self-guided. Photography permitted. Phone: (506) 727-3467. Take N.B. 11 west from Caraquet. The village is located near the town of Bertrand.
- The Acadian Festival takes place annually on August 15. *Tintamarre* and the folk dances take place near and at the old convent on Boulevard St. Pierre in Caraquet. Blessing of the Fleet: first Sunday before August 15.
- The Acadian Museum. Open June, 10 am to 5 pm on weekdays; July and August, 10:00 am to 8:00 pm Monday to Saturday, 1:00 pm to 5:00 pm Sundays. Admission: $1 per adult. Tours are self-guided. Most explanations are in French only, some are bilingual. Photography permitted. The museum is located at 15, Boulevard St. Pierre East near the visitor centre.

Grand Anse

- The Popes Museum. Open end of June to Labour Day, 10:00 am to 6:00 pm daily. Admission: $3.50 per adult All tours are guided. Photography permitted Phone: (506) 727-1713. The museum is located in the village of Grand Anse on N.B. 11.

Kedgwick

- Kedgwick Forestry Museum and

Park. Open July and August, daily 9:00 am to 6:00 pm; mid to end June and September until Labour Day, daily 10:00 am to 5:00 pm. Admission: $5 per adult. Guides are usually available. Photography permitted. From St. Léonard, take N.B. 17 towards Campbellton. Pass through the town of Kedgwick. The Heritage Lumber Camp is just outside town on the right side of the road.

- Kouchibouguac National Park, near Rexton. The park is open year round. From Moncton, take N.B. 11 north. Past the town of Rexton, turn onto N.B. 480, cross N.B. 134 and enter the park. For more information, call (506) 876-2443.

Nictau

- Miller's Canoes. Visits during regular business hours and by appointment. Avoid disappointment by calling (506) 356-2409. Admission free. All tours are guided by the owner. Photography permitted. From Plaster Rock, take N.B. 385 north for about 50 km (31 mi.). In the small community of Nictau, watch for a large number of birdhouses on your right. The shop is located just before them and behind a large cedar-shingled house.

Restigouche Uplands

- Mount Carleton Provincial Park. The park is open year round. Admission free. From Fredericton, take the Trans-Canada (#2) north to Perth-Andover. Here, turn onto N.B. 109 and follow it to Plaster Rock. Turn left at a well-marked intersection onto N.B. 385 and follow the newly constructed road to the park. For more information call (506) 551-1377 or (506) 735-2525.

Richibucto River near Rexton

- Bonar Law Historic Site. Open late June to late September, daily 9:30 am to 4:30 pm. Admission free. Guides are available. Photography permitted. Phone: (506) 523-7615. On N.B. 11, take exit #53 and drive towards Rexton. Cross the bridge and turn left just past the Irving gas station. The historic site is a short

distance on the left side of the road.

Shippagan

- Marine Centre and Aquarium. Open mid-May to mid-September, daily 10:00 am to 6:00 pm. Admission: $5.35 per adult. Tours are self-guided. Staff is available for questions. Photography permitted. Phone: (506) 336-3013. In Shippagan, follow the main road, Boulevard J.D. Gauthier, to a large red brick building. Turn left in front of that building into 9th Street and follow the small street to its end where the Marine Centre is located.

MIRAMICHI RIVER ROUTE

Bartibog

- MacDonald Farm Historic Site. Open late June to late September, daily 9:30 am to 4:30 pm. Admission: $2.25 per adult. Guided tours are available upon request. Photography permitted. Phone: (506) 778-6085; 453-2324. From Newcastle, follow N.B. 11 towards Caraquet for 12.8 km (8 mi.) beyond the junction of N.B. 11 and N.B. 8. The visitor centre of the historic site is located on the right side of the road.

Boiestown

- Central New Brunswick Woodmen's Museum. Open from late May to September, daily 10:00 am to 5:30 pm. Admission: $4.28 per adult. Tours are self-guided, guides are available upon request. Photography permitted. From Fredericton, take N.B. 8 towards Newcastle. The Woodmen's Museum is located in Boiestown on your right. For special events, call (506) 369-7214.
- Miramichi's Irish Festival. Date: Friday to Sunday in mid-July. For more information call (506) 773-5808. Admission: $7 per day; three-day passes are available. Evening concerts are extra. From N.B. 8 North of Newcastle, cross the Miramichi River on the Centennial Bridge (N.B. 11). Follow the road to the exit to C.F.B. Chatham, but turn left. Just beyond the overpass there is a water tower on the right side of the

road with a shamrock on it. The Lord Beaverbrook Arena is beside the tower. Some events take place in nearby buildings.

Doaktown

• Doak Historic Site. Open end of June to end of September, daily 9:30 am to 4:30 pm. Admission: donations accepted. Guided tours available. Photography permitted. Phone: (506) 365-4363; 453-2324. The park is located in the village of Doaktown along N.B. 8.

• Miramichi Salmon Museum. Open June and September, Monday to Saturday 10:00 am to 5:00 pm, Sunday 1:00 pm to 5:00 pm; July and August, Monday to Saturday 10:00 am to 5:30 pm, Sunday 11:00 am to 5:30 pm. Admission: $3 per adult. Tours are self-guided. Photography permitted. Phone: (506) 365-7787. The museum is in the village of Doaktown along N.B. 8.

Douglastown

• Rankin House. Open first week in July to end of August, Monday to Saturday 9:00 am to 5:00 pm, Sunday 1:00 pm to 5:00 pm. Admission free. Donations are accepted. Guides are available upon request. A tour of the house takes about 30 to 45 minutes. Photography permitted. Phone: (506) 773-3448. The house is located on the Prince George Highway in Douglastown.

• Miramichi Folk Song Festival. Date: First week of August. For information and program, call (506) 627-1495 during business hours or (506) 622-1780 after hours, or write to: Miramichi Folk Song Festival, P.O. Box 13, Newcastle, N.B., E1V 3M2. Some shows are free, most cost between $6 and $10 per adult. Photography permitted.

• The Miramichi Highland Gathering. Date: Last weekend in August. Admission: $10 per adult for the Saturday night concert. The regular admission, $2.25, is charged for Sunday afternoon events at Bartibog. All other events are free. Photography permitted. Location: Various around Newcastle. For further details, call Verne Potter at (506) 627-4039 or (506) 627-2511.

OUTDOOR RECREATION

BICYCLING

River Valley Scenic Drive

• Cycl'eau Inc., Edmundston (506) 739-6800.

Fundy Coastal Drive

• Baymount Outdoor Adventure Services, Hillsborough. (506) 734-2660
• Covered Bridge Bicycle Tours, Saint John. (506) 849-9028
• Single Trax Cycles Inc. (506) 652-8729
• The Outdoor Adventure Company, St. Andrews E0G 2X0. 1-800-365-3855 fax (506) 755-6009
• Eastwind Cycle Broadway Café, PO Box 1958, Sussex (506) 433-5414 fax (506) 433-6335

Acadian Coastal Route

• T.F. Sports Impact Ltd., 270 St. Pierre Boulevard West, Caraquet E1W 1A4

Miramichi River Route

• Clearwater Hollow Expeditions, McNamee. (506) 365-7636 or 1-800-563-Trail

BICYCLE RENTALS

River Valley Scenic Drive

• Savages Bicycle, Fredericton. (506) 458-8985
• Waterfront Mountain Bike Rentals, Fredericton. (506) 450-5731

Fundy Coastal Drive

• Alternatives Home & Leisure Ltd., Saint John. (506) 633-1500
• Broadway Cycle & Ski, Sussex. (506) 433-2184
• Fundy Mountain Bike Rentals, Alma (506) 887-2233.
• Granite Town Hotel, St. George. (506) 755-6415. Fax. (506) 755-6009
• Seahawk Enterprises, Grand Manan. (506) 662-3464
• The Pedal Pusher Bike Shop, Sackville. (506) 536-0575

- The Quaco Inn, St. Martins. (506) 833-4772. Fax. (506) 833-2531

Acadian Coastal Route
- Aquamusement, Tracadie/Sheila. (506) 395-9136
- Kouchibouguac National Park Rental Centre. (506) 523-4241, 876-2571

BIRDING

Birding guides and tour operators within New Brunswick:

Fundy Coastal Drive
- Don's Natural History & General Tours, Grand Manan. (506) 662-8801
- Fundy Hiking and Nature Tours, Inc., St. Martins. (506) 833-2534, Fax. (506) 833-2531
- Huntsman Marine Science Centre, St. Andrews. (506) 529-8895
- Inn on the Cove, Saint John. (506) 672-7799
- Hole in the Wall, Basil Small, Grand Manan. (506) 662-3152.
- Naturescape Inc. 1216 Sand Cove Road, St. John (506) 672-7722
- Fundy National Park, Alma (506) 887-6000.
- Island Coast Boat Tours Inc., Grand Manan. (506) 662-8181
- Machias Seal Island Tour, Grand Manan. (506) 662-8552
- Mahnanook Nature Tours, Grand Manan. (506) 662-8650
- Seawatch Tours, Grand Manan. (506) 662-8296
- Sunbury Shores Art and Nature Centre, St. Andrews. (506) 529-3386

Acadian Coastal Route
- Stuart Tingley. Shediac Bridge. (506) 532-0885
- Paul Germain. Acadian Coastal 5D Tours Inc. St. Louis de-Kent E0A 2Z0 T3l (506) 876-4645 fax (506) 876-4645.

BOAT/HOUSEBOAT RENTALS

River Valley Scenic Drive
- Cambridge Village Inn (Party boat), Cambridge-Narrows. (506) 488-3105
- N.B. Sailing Association (Information on Sailing Clubs and lessons). Pauline Wilson, Executive Director, N.B. Sailing Association,. P.O. Box 4005, Station B, Saint John, E2M 5E6. (506) 738-8677, fax (506) 738-8133

Fundy Coastal Drive
- Beaton Aqua Dive and Charter Ltd., St. Andrews. (506) 529-3443
- Eastern Outdoors. Saint John. (506) 634-1530, Toll-free. 1-800-56-kayak. Fax. (506) 634-8253
- Prince Yacht Charters Ltd., St. Andrews. (506) 529-4185
- Houseboat Vacations, Sussex. (506) 433-4801 or (506) 433-1609 (after hours)

Acadian Coastal Route
- Shediac Yacht Charters Ltd., Shediac. (506) 532-2585 or (506) 532-5293

CANOE/KAYAK RENTAL

River Valley Scenic Drive
- Cool Moose 'n Stuff, Clair. (506) 992-2827
- Discovery Adventures, Fredericton. (506) 457-1177, fax (506) 451-2228
- Fredericton Small Craft Aquatic Center, Fredericton. (506) 462-6021; 458-9478 (in season)
- The Bucket Club Outdoor Activity Park, Fredericton, NB (506) 451-9696 (506)451-9889.
- Le Canotier Inc., Saint-Basile. (506) 735-3685, (506) 735-6184 (off season)
- Nackawic Canoe/Kayak Club, Nackawic. (506) 575-2456

Fundy Coastal Drive
- Adventure High Sea Kayaking, Grand Manan. (506) 662-3563
- Eastern Outdoors, Saint John. (506) 634-1530 or 1-800-56Kayak. Fax (506) 634-8253
- Granite Town Hotel, St. George. (506) 755-6415. Fax. (506) 755-6009
- Seascape Kayak Tours Inc., St. Andrews. (506)529-4866

Acadian Coastal Route
- Aquamusement, Tracadie/Sheila. (506) 395-9136
- Centre de Plein Air du Vieux Moulin Inc., Saint-Quentin. (506)

235-1110
- Kedgwick Canoe & Kayak Club, Kedgwick. (506) 284-2201

CANOE RENTALS/GUIDED TOURS

River Valley Scenic Drive
- Don's Hardware Ltd., Plaster Rock. (506) 356-2665
- Don's River View Lodge, Plaster Rock. (506) 356-8351.
- Douglas Development Corp. Ltd., Fredericton. (506) 450-6080
- Eagle ValleyAdventures, Clair. (506) 992-2827
- Echo Restigouche Experience Nature Inc., Kedgwick (506) 284-2022.
- Tobique River Tours, Plaster Rock. (506) 356-2514.
- Kingfisher Lodge, Plaster Rock. (506) 356-2028
- St. Croix Canoe Rentals, McAdam. (506) 784-3309
- Steamers Stop Inn, Gagetown. (506) 488-2903

Fundy Coastal Drive
- B&D Boat and Canoe Rentals Inc., Alma; (506) 887-2115
- Fundy National Park
- Loon Bay Lodge, St. Stephen. (506) 466-1240
- Moores Canoes, St. Stephen. (506) 466-3561
- The Tool Hut, Sussex. (506) 433-6110
- Piskahegan River Co., St. George (506)755-6269.
- Seascape Kayak Tours Inc., St. Andrews (506)529-4866.

Acadian Coastal Route
- Cyrille Albert, Pokemouche. (506) 727-3510
- Jacques Levesque Location de Canot, Charlo. (506) 684-5200
- Kouchibouguac National Park, Kouchibouguac. (506) 876-2443 or (506) 876-4802.
- LeBlanc Rental, Campbellton. (506) 753-6080
- LeBlanc Rental, Dalhousie. (506) 684-4788
- LeBlanc's Rivers & Trails Canoe Outfitters Inc., Bathurst. (506) 548-4326
- Pourvoirie des Hauts Plateaux, Saint John-Baptiste. (506) 284-

2444
- Caraquet, Plage Centre-Ville Ltd. (506) 727-7411

Miramichi River Route
- O'Donnells Canoeing Adventures Ltd., Doaktown (506) 365-7924
- Brad Reilley. Stanley. (506) 367-2117
- Bush and Brook Sports Rental Ltd., Taymouth. (506) 457-1614
- Clearwater Hollow Expeditions, McNamee. 1-800-563-trail (8724) or (506) 365-7636
- Ponds Resort, Ludlow. (506) 369-2612

FISHING

River Valley Scenic Drive
- Fredericton, Kingsclear Outfitters (506) 363-5111 toll free 1-800-501-5111
- Perth-Andover, Carleton Victoria Fish Hatchery (506) 273-2310 toll free 1-800-303-1144
- Oromocto, Guided Atlantic Salmon Fly Fishing Miramichi Gray Rapids Lodge Inc., Blackville (506)357-9784

Fundy Coastal Drive
- Penfield, Interactive Outdoors Limited. (506)755-2699

Acadian Coastal Region
- Pointe-Verte, Pointe Verte Atlas Park (506) 783-3717 or 783-7973

Miramichi
- Newcastle-Miramichi, Upper Oxbow Outdoor Adventures. (506) 622-8834 year round (506) 836-7132.

GOLF COURSES

River Valley Scenic Drive
- Aroostook Valley Golf Club. 18 holes. (207) 476-6501
- Edmundston Golf and Country Club Ltée. 18 holes. (506) 735-3086
- Fredericton Golf and Curling Club. 18 holes. (506) 458-0003
- Gilridge Golf Club. 9 holes executive. (506) 453-1077
- Grand Falls/Grand-Sault, Grand Falls Golfing Ltd. 18 holes. (506) 473-5186

- Hartland, Covered Bridge Golf and Country Club. 18 holes. (506) 375-1112
- Mactaquac Provincial Park Golf Club. Route 105, West of Fredericton. 18 holes. (506) 363-4139
- Minto, Ridgeview Greens Golf and Country Club. 9 holes. (506) 327-3535
- Nackawic Golf and Country Club. 9 holes. (506) 575-8433
- Oromocto, Gage Golf and Curling Association. 18 holes. (506) 357-9343
- Plaster Rock Golf and Curling Club. 9 holes. (506) 356-2402
- Saint-Jacques, Golf Le Patrimoine. 9 holes. (506) 735-4788
- Welsford Golf and Country Club. 9 holes. (506) 486-9917
- Westfield Golf and Country Club. 18 holes. (506) 757-2250

Woodstock
- Woodstock Golf Club. 9 holes. (506) 328-2386/328-4283 (ProShop)

Fundy Coastal Drive
- Alma, Fundy National Park Golf Course. 9 holes. (506) 887-2970
- Campobello Island, Herring Cove Provincial Park Golf Club. 9 holes. (506) 752-2449
- Hampton Country Club Inc. 18 holes. (506) 832-3407
- Memramcook Valley Golf Club. 9 holes. (506) 758-9242
- Moncton, Country Meadows Golf Club. 18 holes. (506) 858-8909
- Lakeside Golf and Country Club. 18 holes. (506) 859-4202
- Magnetic Hill Golf and Country Club. 18 holes. (506) 858-1611
- Moncton Golf and Country Club. 18 holes. (506) 386-3121
- Stonehurst Golf Club. 18 holes. (506) 858-7080/386-8334 (Off season)
- Petitcodiac Valley Golf and Country Club. 14 holes. (506) 756-9924
- Sackville Golf Club. 9 holes. (506) 536-3437
- Saint John, Riverside Country Club. 18 holes. (506) 847-7545
- Rockwood Park Golf Course. 18 holes. (506) 658-2933/658-2966 (Aquatic Range)

- St. Andrews, Algonquin Golf Course. 27 holes. (506) 529-3062
- St. Stephen Golf Club. 9 holes. (506) 466-5336
- Sussex Golf and Curling Club. 18 holes. (506) 433-6493

Acadian Coastal Route
- Bathurst, Gowan Brae Golf and Country Club. 18 holes. (506) 546-2707
- Bouctouche, Golf Bouctouche 14 Holes. (506) 743-9907
- Campbellton, Restigouche Golf and Country Club. 18 holes. (506) 789-7628
- Pokemouche, Golf Pokemouche Ltée. 18 holes. (506) 727-3577
- Saint-Ignace Golf Course. 18 holes. (506) 876-3737
- Saint-Quentin Golf Club. 9 holes. (506) 235-2578
- Shediac, Pine Needles Golf and Country Club. 27 holes. (506) 532-4634
- St. Margaret's James Park Golf Club. 9 holes. (506) 778-8547

Miramichi River Route
- Doaktown, Old Mill Pond Golf and Country Club. 9 holes. (506) 365-7584
- Durham Bridge, Riverbend Golf and Fishing Club. 9 holes. (506) 452-7277
- Newcastle, Miramichi Golf and Country Club. 18 holes. (506) 622-2068

HIKING GUIDES AND TOUR OPERATORS

River Valley Scenic Drive
- Backcountry Adventures, Fredericton. (506) 363-2316
- ECO Tours, Fredericton. (506) 452-0995

Fundy Coastal Drive
- Baymount Outdoor Adventures, Hillsborough. (506) 734-2660. (506) 383-4881
- Don's Natural History & General Tours, Grand Manan. (506) 662-8801
- Fundy Hiking and Nature Tours Inc., St. Martins. (506) 833-2534. Fax: (506) 833-1112
- Hole-in-the-Wall Park, Grand Manan (506) 662-3152.

- Starboard Tours Ltd., Saint John. (506) 633-7525, 662-8545 (seasonal)

Miramichi River Route
- Clearwater Hollow Expeditions, McNamee. (506) 365-7636, 1-800-563-trail

OTHER HIKING

- Experimental Forest, Université de Moncton. Centre Universitaire St. Louis Maillet. Edmundston. (506) 737-5238 or 737-5068
- Fundy Model Forest, Sussex. Tel. (506) 432-2806. Fax. (506) 432-2807

NATIONAL PARKS

Fundy Coastal Drive
- Fundy National Park. Founded in 1950, the park offers activities as diverse as camping, hiking, biking, boating, lawn bowling, golfing, and swimming. The park is open year round. Admission: vehicle entrance permits are required from mid-May to mid-October. Fees are $6.00 per day. From Sussex, take the Trans-Canada (#2) towards Moncton, then turn onto N.B. 114 and follow it for 25 km (16 mi.) to the northwest entrance of the park. For more information, call (506) 887-6000. Fundy National Park, P.O. Box 40, Alma, NB, E0A 1B0, or call (506) 887-6000. Fax: (506) 887-6008

Acadian Coastal Route
- Kouchibouguac National Park, Kouchibouguac, Kent County, New Brunswick. E0A 2A0. Tel: (506) 876-2443. Fax: (506) 876-4802
- Petit Témis Interprovincial Linear Park. A 60 km (40 mi) new bicycle trail links Edmundston, New Brunswick and Cabano, Quebec. This level trail was completed in 1995 and is known as the Petit Témis Interprovincial Linear Park. In part a "rail trail", it leads along the shores of the Temiscouata Lake and the beautiful Madawaska River. For more information, call (506) 739-1992.

PROVINCIAL PARKS/BEACHES

River Valley Scenic Drive
- Oak Point Campground, supervised beach, picnicking, scenic lighthouse, canoeing. On scenic River Road (Route 102). 48 km (30 mi.) north of Saint John. (506) 468-2266
- Grand Lake Campground, supervised beach, boat launch, windsurfing, canoeing, bird-watching, 1.5 km. accessible trail. On Route 690, 65 km (40 mi.) from Fredericton. (506) 385-2919
- Mactaquac, Mouth of Keswick. Large campground, 18-hole championship golf course, licensed lodge, supervised beaches and recreation program, marinas, boat launches, hiking trails, 1.5 km. wheelchair accessible trail around beaver pond, windsurfing, canoeing, fishing, picnicking. On Route 105, 24 km (15 mi.) west of Fredericton. (506) 363-3011
- Woolastook. Picnicking, boat launch, wind surfing, canoeing, fishing. Large, privately operated campground, waterslides, miniature golf, wildlife park. Kings Landing Historical Settlement nearby. On Route 2 (TCH) 30 km (18 mi.) west of Fredericton. (506) 363-5410
- Les Jardins de la République. Large campground, antique auto museum, supervised pool and recreation program, tennis courts, picnicking, walking trails, theatre, canoeing. Adjacent to the New Brunswick Botanical Garden. North of Edmundston at Saint-Jacques on Route 2 (TCH). (506) 735-4871 or 735-2525 (district office)
- Lakeside. Recreational park, campground, picnic area, non-supervised beach. On route 2 (TCH), Waterborough. (506) 488-2532
- Saint-Léonard. Campground, picnic area near route 2 (TCH). (506) 423-6987
- North Lake. Primitive campground, non-supervised beach, picnic area. 20 km west of Canterbury on route 122. (506) 279-2012
- Spednic Lake. Primitive campground, picnic area, boat launches, canoeing, 4.8 km. hiking

trail. West of McAdam on route 630. (506) 279-2012 (district office)

Fundy Coastal Drive

- St. Croix Provincial Park. Canoeing: the scenic St. Croix Heritage River System that builds the southwestern border between Canada and the United States is ideal for canoeing. Spednic Lake and the St. Croix are shaped by the last glaciation and native peoples occupied the area for centuries. Camping is available at St. Croix Provincial Park near McAdam and on small islands in the river system that can be reached only by boat.
- The Rocks, Hopewell Cape. Famous flowerpot rocks, spectacular tidal action, interpretive signs and guides, walking trail, bird-watching, picnicking, restaurant. On Route 114, between Moncton and Fundy National Park. (506) 734-3429 (district office)
- New River Beach. Long salt water beach, hiking trails, ocean kayaking, camping, annual sand building contest. On Route 1, 40 km (25 mi.) west of Saint John. (506) 755-3804
- The Anchorage. Campground on the ocean, hiking, beachcombing, bird-watching, bird blinds on migratory bird sanctuary, nearby whale-watching excursions. Route 776 on Grand Manan Island. (506) 662-3215
- Oak Bay. Supervised beach, camping. On Route 1, 8 km (5 mi.) east of U.S. border near St. Stephen. (506) 466-2661
- Herring Cove Provincial Park and Campobello International Park, Campobello Island. Nine-hole golf course and lodge, licensed dining, camping, hiking trails, beach-combing. Via U.S. Route 1. Campobello Provincial Park. (506) 752-2396. Camping: (506) 752-7010 Golfing: (506) 752-2449

Acadian Coastal Route

- Mount Carleton. Large wilderness park, campground, backcountry camping and hiking trail system, 0.8 km trail accessible with assistance, fishing, canoeing, beach, wildlife observation.

Sweeping views from the summit across the Appalachian Mountains canoeing the routes taken by native peoples and the missionaries from France. Cross Country and highland skiing. Route 385, 84 km (52 mi.) north of Plaster Rock, or off Route 180, 43 km (27 mi.) east of St-Quentin. Mount Carleton discovery highway route 17. (506) 235-2025 or 735-2525 (district office)

- Sugarloaf. The wooded campground has 65 serviced sites mostly in wooded or semi-wooded terrain. Tennis courts, hiking, chair-lift ride, licensed lodge and patio, winter sports complex. Sugarloaf offers a wide variety of downhill and cross country ski trails and excellent canoeing and fishing is provided by the Restigouche River. Off Route 11 at Campbellton. P.O. Box 639, Campbellton, N.B. E3N 3H1. (506) 789-2392/2366
- Pokeshaw Scenic lookout, cormorant nesting site, wind and wave-carved shoreline. On Route 11, 35 km (22 mi.) east of Bathurst. (506) 395-8094 or 395-4137 (district office)
- Maisonnette Beach, warm shallow water, bird-watching, windsurfing, 2.4 km (1.5 mi.) sandbar. Off route 11, 8 km (5 mi.) east on Route 320. (506) 395-8094 or 395-4137 (district office)
- Val-Comeau. Supervised beach, campsites on water, bird-watching, windsurfing. Off Route 11, 8 km (5 mi.) east on Route 320. (506) 395-8094 Tracadie-Sheila
- Neguac. Picnic area, beach, boat launch, observation tower, bird-watching. South of Neguac off Route 11. (506) 627-4049 (district office)
- Parlee Beach, Shediac. Campground, large supervised salt water beach, annual sand sculpture contest, windsurfing, triathlon, sand tennis, volleyball and touch football tournaments. Off Route 15 at Shediac Resort Area. (506) 533-3363
- Murray Beach, Murray Corner. Campground on the ocean, beach, bird-watching. On Route 955, 15 km (9.3 mi.) north of Cape Tormentine. (506) 538-2628
- Kellys Beach, Kouchibouguac.

- Supervised, 6.5 km long
- Lagoon at Kelly's Beach. Supervised, 17 km long.
- Charlo. Eel River Bar. Supervised, 1.25 km long.
- Cap-Pélé. Sandy Beach. Unsupervised, 8 km long.

Miramichi River Route
- The Enclosure picnic area, significant historic site and campground. On Route 8.7 km (4.3 mi.) west of Newcastle. (506) 627-4071
- Escuminac Saltwater beach, windsurfing, bird-watching, picnicking. Off Route 117. 5 km (3 mi.) east of Escuminac. (506) 627-4070 (district office)

SCENIC CRUISES

Fundy Coastal Drive
- Partridge Island Boat Tours, Saint John. (506) 635-0782
- Starboard Tours, Saint John. (506) 633-7525 or (506) 662-8545 (seasonal)
- Lake Retreat Outfitters and Charters, Saint John. (506) 636-0130.
- Cline Marine Inc, Deer Island. (506) 747-2287 or 1-800-567-5880.

Acadian Coastal Route
- Carrefour de la mer, Caraquet. (506) 727-3637, fax (506) 727-1726
- Cocagne Marina, Cocagne. (506) 576-9256
- "Chaleur Phantom" Tourboat, Dalhousie. (506) 684-4722
- Sunshine Cruises, Campbellton. (506) 789-7700
- Traversier P.T.C. Ltée., Caraquet. (506) 727-4615
- "Heart to Heart" Charter Services Ltd., Pointe-du-Chêne. (506) 532-3558.
- Marina de Bas-Caraquet. (506) 727-4787

Miramichi River Route
- Miramichi Boat Charter Inc., Newcastle. (506) 622-5585 (June–September). Fax (506) 228-3688

River Valley Scenic Drive
- Mutch's Riverboat Cruises, Perth Andover. (506) 273-6662
- Pioneer Princess 1/2, Fredericton.

(506) 458-5558

SCUBA DIVING

Diving information and services to scuba divers:

River Valley Scenic Drive
- Aqua Nuts. Lac-Baker. (506) 992-3705

Acadian Coastal Route
- Aqua Bulle. Bas-Caraquet. (506) 727-4228
- Atlas Park. Pointe Verte. (506) 783-7973
- Blue Cove Sea Urchins Inc. Anse-Bleue. (506) 732-5683, fax (506) 732-5238
- Cote Nord Dive Centre. Beresford. (506) 542-1011, fax (506) 542-1019

Fundy Coastal Drive
- Beatons Aqua Dive and Charters Ltd., St. Andrews. (506) 529-3443
- Burdens Service Systems Ltd.. Moncton. (506) 859-4098

WHALE-WATCHING

Fundy Coastal Drive
- Grand Manan, Sealand Adventures Ltd. (506) 662-8130
- Deer Island, Sense the Sea. (506) 662-8130.

Acadian Coastal Region
- Caraquet, Sea of Adventure Inc. (506) 727-2727 toll free 1-800-704-3966.
- Campobello Island, Cline Marine Inc. (506) 529-4188 (Reservation) or (506) 747-2287 (Home Office)
- Deer Island, Cline Marine Inc. (506) 747-0114 (Reservation) or (506) 747-2287 (Home Office) toll free 1-800-567-5880.
- Fredericton, Atlantic Marine Wildlife Tours Ltd.. (506) 459-7325
- Grand Manan Island, Ocean Search. (506) 662-8488
- Grand Manan Island, Island Coast Boat Tours. (506) 662-8181
- Grand Manan Island, Seawatch. (506) 662-8552
- Saint John, Eastern Outdoors. (506) 634-1530, Toll-free. 1-800-56-kayak. Fax (506) 634-8253

- St. Andrews, Cline Marine Inc..
  (506) 529-4188 (Reservation) or
  (506) 747-2287 (Home Office)
- St. Andrews, Fundy Tide Runners
  (506) 524-4481.
- St. Andrews, Quoddy Link Marine
  (506) 529-2600.

NATURE EXPLORATION

Fundy Coastal Drive
- Baymount Outdoor Adventures,
  Hillsborough, (506) 734-2660.
- River Marsh Tours, Darlings Island,
  Hampton (506) 832-1990
- Fundy National Park (506) 887-
  6000
- Sunbury Shores Arts and Nature
  Centre, St. Andrews (Children's
  Program). (506) 529-3386

Acadian Coastal Route
- Peat Bog Interpretation Boardwalk,
  Miscou Island.
- 5D Tours/Ecotourism Inc.,
  Cocagne. (506) 576-1994.
- Caraquet Oat Farming. Les Blancs
  d'Acadie (506) 727-5952

River Valley Scenic Drive
- The Tree House Walking/
  Interpretation, Fredericton. (506)
  452-1339.
- Gagetown guided tour (506) 488-
  2903.
- Miramichi Boat Tour (506) 622-
  2244 (506) 778-0900

PHOTOGRAPHY

River Valley Scenic Drive
- Kingston Peninsula. Freeman
  Patterson/Doris Mowry Photo
  Workshops. June/July/October.
  (506) 763-2271

Fundy Coastal Drive
- Adventure High Sea Kayaking,
  Grand Manan. (506) 662-3563, fax
  (506) 662-8392

River Valley Scenic Drive
- Discovery Adventures, Fredericton.
  (506) 457-1177, fax (506) 451-
  2228

HAYRIDES

Miramichi River Route
- Double D. Stables, Chatham. (506)

622-0621

HORSEBACK RIDING

River Valley Scenic Drive
- LTD Stables, Nackawic. (506) 575-
  8164
- Royal Road Riding Stables,
  Fredericton. (506) 452-0040 or
  (506) 450-3059

Fundy Coastal Drive
- Broadleaf Tourist Farm, Hopewell
  Hill. (506) 882-2349, fax (506)
  882-2075
- Circle Square Ranch, Sussex. (506)
  432-6362

Acadian Coastal Route
- Drinkers of the Wind, Dundee.
  (506) 826-3620

Miramichi River Route
- Limekiln Farm Riding Stables,
  Stanley. (506) 367-1080 or (506)
  367-2159 (Home)

RAFTING

Fundy Coastal Drive
- Eastern Outdoors, Saint John.
  (506) 634-1530. Toll-free. 1-800-
  56-kayak. Fax (506) 634-8253

RAPPELLING

Fundy Coastal Drive
- A unique experience awaits the
  adventurous traveler at Cape
  Enrage, a short distance from
  Fundy National Park. The sheer
  cliffs and overhangs are ideal for
  rappelling. Experienced guides will
  show you "the ropes". Call Cape
  Enrage Adventures at (506) 887-
  2273 or (506) 856-6081.

ROCK & ICE CLIMBING

Fundy Coastal Drive
- Fundy Rock and Ice Climbing
  School Inc., Saint John. (506) 432-
  6388. Fax (506) 633-5129

INDEX

PHOTO CREDITS

Legend: Top - T; Centre - C; Bottom - B Photography by **H.A. Eiselt** with the following exceptions: **Steven Isleifsen**, pp. 37C; 38T; **New Brunswick Tourism— Brian Atkinson**, pp. 43T; 20T; 27T; 31B; 34; **Gilles Daigle**, pp. 17B; 36T; **M.J. DeWolfe**, p. 45C; **André Gallant**, pp. 17T; 19C; 22T; 24T; 49B; 82B; 83T; 108B; **Louise and Mike Jessop**, p. 10T; **Keith Vaughan**, p. 37T; **New Brunswick Tourism,** pp. 15T; 19T; 22B; 28; 46B; 69T; 109B; 120T&B; 121; 122T; 123C&B; 124T; 154T; **Patrick Polchies**, p. 14B; **Randy Simon**, pp. 11B; 12; **Keith Vaughan**, pp. 2T; 29T; 68T; **Lynn Wigginton**, pp. 2B; 39B; 40; 41; 42